Not Alone

A Christ-centered recovery process
for women who have experienced
physical, emotional, or sexual trauma

Anne Richardson

A.M. Richardson Publishing
San Diego, California 92124

©2019 Anne Richardson
Adapted from *Not Alone* ©2016 Anne Richardson

www.amrichardsonpublishing.com
www.spiritualdirectionandtrauma.com

Unless otherwise indicated, all Scripture quotations are taken from the Holy Bible, New International Version®. NIV®, Copyright © 1973, 1978, 1984 by International Bible Society. Used by permission of Zondervan. All rights reserved worldwide.

Scripture quotations marked (MSG) are taken from *THE MESSAGE*, Copyright © 1993, 1994, 1995, 1996, 2000, 2001, 2002. Used by permission of NavPress Publishing Group.

Cover Design: Vicki Hesterman
Cover photo: Ron Richardson

Printed by Print Services of Point Loma Nazarene University, San Diego, California.

ISBN 978-1-7329544-1-0

This is dedicated to all the "hers" who have suffered from trauma.

Here are testimonials from women who have journeyed with me in *Not Alone*. They have given me permission to share their stories. Their names have been changed.

"I enjoyed the gentle, gracious and supportive approach to healing as churches don't always get this right. Seeing how Jesus feels for me, when I was emotionally abused in my marriage, has created a shift in my thinking. My trust in God has been growing since the trauma damaged my relationship with Him. I have an elevated self-esteem and confidence from being a part of this group." Jessica

"I was kidnapped and raped at gunpoint when I was a young woman. I can't say enough about this group and how much I appreciate the opportunity to participate in it. My relationship with Jesus, God, and the Holy Spirit has changed dramatically. I know God loves me, even though I was not spared from the pain. The teachings and practices on shame and fear spoke to me so loudly. I know the internal changes that were made in me, because of God and this group, will be long lasting." JH

"I suffered from the effects of sexual trauma at the hands of my father. In this group, I loved how the in-depth look at the Bible stories along with contemplation helped me look at my trauma from a new perspective. What I learned in a powerful way is the more my heart, mind, and being are filled with God's love, the more I am compelled to forgive others. It doesn't mean being a doormat or letting people abuse me. My quest for meaning and longing for peace can only come from God. Being more like Him meant I needed to forgive as He does. I was able to forgive both my parents, especially my mom who did nothing to protect us kids. The shackles that kept me in bondage melted away. I can honestly say...*I am free.*" Beth

"I have been in therapy and in spiritual direction, but I have grown so much more by being a part of this group process. My anxiety is less noticeable and not out of control when I get triggered. I loved the Imaginative prayer exercise as they opened up my ability to connect with God. I felt very little trust towards God before I started the group. After going through this, I know He is really there for me." Teresa

"I didn't feel valued because of the trauma by my mother. I felt unworthy. Being a part of this group and helped me know in my heart that I am God's Beloved daughter. My prayer life deepened from being a part of this group. As I practiced Soaking prayer, I had some tender, loving moments with Jesus. I even felt more love for my husband." Emily

"My mother died when I was young leaving a feeling of emptiness in me. I have been a Christian for a long time, but I never knew that Jesus goes out of His way for me. Learning how to do Imaginative prayer has helped me experience more of His love for me. That was so powerful!" Terry

Contents

Preface

I am a survivor of molestation.

Shame, fear and doubt held me back in my life until I truly experienced Him. God has been slowly stitching up the wound in me created by the trauma. He is the one who has and still is transforming me. His unending grace and extravagant love fill me with a sense of belonging. I know in my heart I am His Beloved daughter.

As a spiritual director and mentor, I have journeyed with many women who desire intimacy and healing from God. Sadly, many tell me that they know in their head that God loves them but deep down, they don't really believe it in their hearts. This transformational process has helped women truly know they are His Beloved. You are welcome to come on this journey of becoming the beautiful, beloved woman that God created you to be.

Abuse is about power and control. Someone who was stronger, older, or in authority violated another human being to assert control and power. Statistics indicate that sexual abuse happens in one out of four women, and it is often perpetrated by someone the victim knew and trusted. Many women have also been wounded by emotional and physical trauma. Trauma can create a wound that the victim will try to fill with *something* or *someone* for the rest of their lives. Only God can truly satisfy our souls. I know this sounds like a pat answer but it's true. Abuse also robs a person of faith, hope and trust in God. Becoming aware of what truly blocks our faith, hope and love can open the door to a deeper, more satisfying relationship with Him.

We can choose to deny our pain, stuff it, ignore it, numb it or fix it in an unhealthy way, or we can choose to face it, explore it, accept it, express it in a healthy way and bring it before God. I am inviting you to choose the latter. We don't need to remain victims or remain in a victim mentality. We can experience healing, be empowered, move on and live in peace, love and freedom. It is normal to experience fear, anxiety, worry, discontent, or even hatred, and yet we don't need to stay there. Jesus said that He came to give us the abundant life (John10:10). I believe that He was talking about the interior life, the fruits of the Spirit:

love, joy, peace, patience, kindness, goodness, faithfulness and self-control (Galatians 5:22). This kind of life is open to all.

This spiritual recovery process requires spending time alone in silence and engaging in various spiritual practices with Jesus, the Great Physician and the Wounded Healer. I use the analogy of having a broken shoulder. In order to fully heal, you must spend time with the Physical Therapist and the Physician. You can choose to learn more about the shoulder, how it heals and what to do. You can also learn about the Physician and know a lot about him. But in order to truly heal, you need to just be with Him, feeling His presence, engaging in spiritual practices. Otherwise it's just head knowledge. Information is good and necessary, however, it's not enough. Sadly, many people know a lot about God, but don't truly experience Him or feel His love in their daily lives. This is where I see women get stuck.

You can use this book alone or with a therapist, mentor or spiritual director or in a group. I will share various spiritual practices to try inside of group healing sessions (which I will refer to as "group" if you are in one) and during your time at home with God, which allows healing, transformation, and experiencing His love. Try to be open since some of these may be new to you. Many of these practices come from both Catholic and Protestant traditions and are based in the scriptures. It saddens me when I see fighting and quarrels among these two religions. Regardless of theology differences, both believe in God, Jesus and the Holy Spirit as the Divine Trinity. *Jesus came for relationship, not a religion.*

Each chapter also includes reflection exercises to help you explore, gain insight and awareness of the desires of your heart, and see how the manifestations of trauma interfere or block this loving relationship with God, yourself and others.

This is not a "quick fix," as healing and transformation are a lifelong process. I tell others I am a WIP (Work in Progress) who loves God and loves Jesus. Be patient and trust God with the process. **The key is to spend time with Him.** God created you in His image. He desires to have a loving, intimate relationship with you. He wants to heal your deepest wounds and restore you to truly know that you are the beloved daughter He created you to be.

You *can* experience this deeper relationship with Him. I welcome you to this journey! You are not alone.

Introduction

This spiritual recovery process is designed for women who are ready to allow God to enter in and heal the broken places in order to live more freely as the Beloved. This book is created to complement more formal therapy, AA, Celebrate Recovery, healing prayer, and other types of support groups. It is not a substitute for counseling. In my experience, therapy was insightful and gave me knowledge and insight that I needed. However, spending time alone with God and with these practices has gradually brought a closer walk with God and deeper healing into my life

This recovery process can be done in a small group or in a one-on-one relationship with a spiritual director or mentor. The benefits of being in a group include learning from one another and knowing that we are not alone. The benefits of doing this one-on-one include having more time to explore oneself and being able to go at your own pace. You may choose to have a spiritual director, mentor or therapist in addition to meeting in the group. A spiritual director is someone who comes alongside another to listen, pray, and ask open-ended questions to encourage someone to deepen their experiences of God and grow closer to Him. Most spiritual directors are trained and certified. A mentor may also listen, encourage, pray and teach from their life experiences.

Chapters 1 and 2 will cover getting started and being the Beloved. Chapters 3-10 each discuss a common manifestation of trauma: trust, shame, over-reacting in anger, fear, worry, anxiety, control, envy, idolatry, addictions and relationships. Chapter 11 talks about grief. Chapter 12 is about forgiveness and letting go. Appendixes at the end of the book include a leader's guide, group application, covenant agreement and guidelines for writing your spiritual journey. Although there is some variation, each chapter includes a brief introduction of a manifestation caused by trauma (issues that block our emotional and spiritual maturity), a biblical story, a true story, spiritual practices, reflection exercises, and creative practices.

I will share true stories throughout the workbook with you from other survivors, as well as my own. Their names have been changed to protect their identity. You will learn how

God intervened in our lives and how His healing presence was experienced. If, however, reading this information or sharing your story is upsetting, then **please read or share only what is comfortable for you**. I will also present stories from women in the Bible who received Jesus' compassion and healing.

Almost every chapter will include several spiritual practices which are *tools* that allow God's transformational healing. The key is to be open and surrender to God as opposed to trying to make it happen. The personal reflection worksheets will help you gain insight into your feelings, motives and desires. The key here is to **slow down**, to be still, and create the space for God to enter in. We can learn to experience more of God when we practice silence and solitude.

> The Lord said, "Go out and stand on the mountain in the presence of the Lord, for the Lord is about to pass by." Then a great and powerful wind tore the mountains apart and shattered the rocks before the Lord, but the Lord was not in the wind. After the wind there was an earthquake, but the Lord was not in the earthquake. After the earthquake came a fire, the Lord was not in the fire. And after the fire came a gentle whisper.
>
> 1 Kings 19:11-12

Jesus is our role model for creating silence and solitude with God. He started His ministry with 40 days of silence and solitude in the desert (Luke 4:1-12). He often retreated to pray and be alone with God (Mark 1:35). He encouraged people to go into their quiet room to pray (Matt. 6:6). He knew who He was and had such a deep, loving relationship with His father that they were one.

Jesus knew the scriptures. He also served the people. In His ministry, He did many things: taught, evangelized, cast out demons, healed the sick, and fed the poor. Most of our churches today encourage service and Bible study, which are truly a part of being a Christ-follower. Yet Jesus also spent time in silence and solitude with God. I believe this practice is becoming a lost art in our society. Jesus served out of being the beloved and out of true love for God as evidenced by their close, genuine relationship. I have seen in others and in myself how Jesus enters in and provides deeper healing when we will give Him time and space in solitude.

Silence and solitude is not about emptying your mind. It is about quieting your mind, slowing down, and putting aside the internal chatter so you can listen to God. Silence and solitude is not about being alone, as God is with you always.

Please have realistic expectations. *This process may stir up emotions in you, which is normal. You are not crazy. God may be inviting you to a deeper place of healing.* Recovery is the slow work of God in you. This usually is not accomplished in 12 sessions; hopefully, however, you will begin to experience more intimacy with God, truly being the beloved and having more freedom in your life.

There are many practices to try. If one doesn't work, then try another. There is a lot of material in this book and you can do as much or as little as you want to. Some women said they just went where they needed to go with God, spending more time in one chapter and less in another. That is ok, too. Some women told me they referred back to the material long after group was done.

Negative emotions and struggles are a part of life and yet will be easier to deal with when we have an authentic relationship with God. Love will be the emotion that permeates. My internal struggles are not gone, yet I notice I am not "spinning in my head" as much as I once did, or taking things personally. I have more confidence and courage to do the inner work and share this all with you. I am able to live in more freedom and that peace that surpasses understanding (Phil.4:7).

Coming alongside women and witnessing how God has brought healing and new meaning to their lives brings me joy. I invite you to come along with us in this journey of healing and restoration. He loves you and desires a relationship with you, more than you know!

Chapter One
Getting Started

Creating the Space Inside and Outside of the Group

Spend time writing and reflecting on your story prior to your group starting or meeting with your spiritual director/mentor (see Appendix B). If you are a leader, please see the Leaders guide in Appendix A for suggestions. Writing your story helps you see how God has been active in your life, whether you felt His presence or not. You may want to reflect on your story throughout the group process. Prepare to plan to share highlights with the group on the first day. Again, please share only what is comfortable. I will share my story with you as well. Sharing our stories helps us connect with one another and realize that we are not alone.

To create safety inside of group, it is important that you commit to regularly attend for your sake and for others, except for health related or other serious situations that may arise. Please e-mail or call the leader if you are not able to attend.

Please respect confidentiality. What everyone shares must stay in the room. Your leader will respect confidentiality except in the case of admitting to child abuse, elder abuse or causing serious physical harm to yourself. If you would like more detail about these exceptions, please ask to speak with your group leader one-on-one.

Finally, please be on time, preferably about five minutes early so the group can start and end on time.

It is necessary to create a sacred space during group time. Be open and compassionate as someone is sharing. Please do not cross talk or give advice or make the story about you, which is sometimes a natural empathetic reaction but gets off-track. Hold each person as a beloved child of God. When you experience difficulty listening to others, as it may stir your own painful story, try to put it aside and continue listening. Later, go to God, or a safe person, counselor, or spiritual director and talk about what was difficult for you.

We want to be open, warm and loving to the person who is sharing. We are neither above them (arrogant) nor below them (self-loathing). We try not to judge or criticize. Try to "hold differences" by seeing people as different from us, not right/wrong, good/bad, etc. It is O.K. to be different; it is O.K. to be you and let others be themselves. We are all children of God. We are all works in progress. And we are all His beloved.

We will be sharing our stories with each other, which can be quite healing. As we listen to others, we realize we are not alone. *If, however, this is upsetting for you, then please share only what is comfortable.*

The group is not psychotherapy, a replacement for therapy, or a "Quick Fix." It is best used to supplement therapy or other kind of support group (e.g. AA, Al-anon, covenant groups, healing prayer). If something is triggered in you, please see your therapist.

Creating a sacred space for yourself outside of group time is important. **The key is time spent with God.** It is like dating. In order to get to know someone, we need to spend time with them. When I first met my husband, I cleared the calendar to be with him. I couldn't wait to see him and my heart ached while we were away. I encourage you to *try* to have that attitude toward your time with God. It might be difficult at first, but with some time, I believe you will experience His love and healing in your life. Today, I find that if a day goes by without spending time with God, *I miss Him.*

In order to truly experience God's healing, begin by setting aside a minimum of 30 minutes every day for silence and reflection. Find a quiet, safe place where you can be alone with Him. This may be in your home where you can close the door, turn off the phone and remove any distractions (T.V., internet, pets, people, and food). It could be a quiet, outdoor setting. You can practice the various prayer exercises, spiritual disciplines, and reflection papers during your alone time. These are tools which allow God's healing in your life. If one practice does not work for you, then try another.

Journaling is a spiritual discipline. It helps summarize the thoughts going on in our heads by writing them down. I find it easier to have clarity when I journal, particularly when I need to release some of my thoughts. Lines are provided in the workbook, although you may want to have more space, so you may wish to have a journal to write in.

Silence and solitude are spiritual disciplines. Jesus started His ministry with 40 days of silence and solitude in the desert. He often retreated from the crowds and his ministry to be alone with God. Being alone can be scary for some of you at first. Yet know that He is with you and you are not alone. This is about solitude with God, not loneliness. This is not about deprivation but being with the One who loves you the most.

Unfortunately, with all the busy-ness and noise in our lives, it is difficult to quiet ourselves and listen to God's voice. Work, children, T.V., texting, Facebook, and "monkey mind" all distract us in today's world. "Monkey mind" is a term therapists use to describe all that chattering going on in our heads. If you are not used to having silent time, it will take practice, and will get easier over time. Don't beat yourself up if you miss a day as His mercies are new every morning. A time of silence and solitude is not about emptying your mind; it's about putting your thoughts, worries, spinning, fantasizing, daydreaming aside so you can be open and present to hear and experience God.

Here are some practical suggestions:

- Pick a quiet, safe place.
- Let the time be a gift to yourself with no expectations. God is present with you even if you don't feel it a certain time or if you don't hear something from Him.
- Remove distractions. I have a prayer room and I close the door. I turn off the phone.
- Offer yourself to God as you are. Just be you.
- Get comfortable.
- Lay your hands open and upward on your lap. Close your eyes. Breathe in slowly. Exhale slowly.
- Focus on your breathing before you start your practice. Breathe in God, breathe out whatever your troubles are. Breathe in Jesus, breathe out your agenda. Breathe in the Holy Spirit, breathe out compassion for yourself.
- Focus on an image of God or Jesus if you choose, as if you are sitting with Him now.
- When other thoughts enter in, and they will, try putting them in an imaginary cupboard. Return to your breathing or the spiritual practice.
- Try journaling your experiences of God, your awareness of His presence.
- Express gratitude to God for the time, even if it was difficult or you didn't feel His presence. He was there with you.

Sharing Our Stories

Sharing your story is a part of your healing journey. Just releasing what happened to cause such pain can be healing in and of itself. I encourage you to reflect back over your story to see how God was present with you even though you may not have felt it. I know God did not cause my molestation, but He was there…crying and mourning. I may never why this happened or why He didn't stop it. I do know I have grown through all this. Now I feel called to share my story with others and to come alongside them as a listening companion so they too can live more freely as the Beloved.

I hope you will share your story. I want to share mine with you.

My Story

A major turning point happened in my life on my 50th birthday. A leader in my church, someone I thought was my friend, called me on the phone after my birthday party and attacked my integrity. It felt like a stiletto was jabbed into my stomach and twisted. I slowly shrank into a fetal position.

I couldn't understand why this was so devastating to me. On a scale of one to ten, the situation probably rated a five. I made it a 10. She and I did talk it out and were able to hear both sides of the story. We forgave each other, but I couldn't reconcile the relationship. I couldn't understand why I still felt so devastated. This was the start of a deeper journey with God and with myself. God invited me to enter into a time alone with Him, to discover and to face my childhood wounds and how this manifested into my adult life. He wanted me to love Him with my whole heart, mind, soul and strength. He wanted to fill me with His love and get my identity in Him, not other people. He wanted to spend time with me. I stepped out of the ministry, entered into therapy and went into the desert with God.

I was born into a good, well-intentioned family. My father was moral, hardworking and a good provider for the family. He also had anger issues, was a rage-aholic and a functioning alcoholic. He took his anger out mostly on my mother, although my sisters and I often bore the brunt of his verbal angry outbursts. As the youngest child, I would run away and hide in order to feel safe. I believed as a young child that anger was bad.

When I was nine years old, my grandmother moved into our home. She was slowly dying of cancer. She moved into my bedroom and I stayed in a room with my sister. I loved my grandmother and I felt loved by her. She called me her "Little Honey" and I called her "Big Honey." I have fond memories of camping with her in Yosemite. She made me a fishing pole out of a stick and I caught a fish! She was so proud of me. She had a tough side, too. One day a big bear came into our camp. I started screaming my head off. She threw a rock at that bear and chased him out of the camp. I will never forget that. I was happy to give her my room as she lay dying. She passed away when I was 10. I grieved the loss of my "Big Honey."

My mother was warm and nurturing. She took me to church and was the spiritual leader in our home. My mother's attention was focused on taking care of her dying mother. My sisters were much older than me and into normal teenage activities. Although this was not intentional from my family, so much was going on in their lives that I felt invisible as a little girl. So I would go to the Berger's home in my neighborhood. Lindsey was my best friend.

The Berger's home was fun. Mrs. Berger was young and would take us to go get Slurpees. She would drive as fast over the bumpy roads as if we were going on a rollercoaster. In those days, we didn't wear seat belts or sit in car seats. We would scream and laugh as she drove us over the rolling dips in the road.

I remember Mrs. Berger taking us places, like Belmont Park. That was the first time I ever went on the roller coaster. I almost lost my stomach and vowed to never ride that again. They had a swimming pool in their backyard and I loved to swim more than anything. Lindsey and I would play for hours, dressing up, pretending we were the characters on our favorite TV show. There were many other little girls who gathered regularly at their house and we would play with Barbies and dress up. This "fun" and "attention" is what I needed as a little girl. As I reflect back, I now describe it as a Hansel and Gretel story -- a house full of fun, chocolate, candy, play… and a deceptive, evil witch. In this case, the witch was Lindsey's father.

I experienced several incidences of molestation when I was between 8-10 years old. Here is one:

I was sitting on the couch, frozen still in fear, like a fawn that senses a wolf nearby. He put his fingers down my pajama pants. I couldn't move. I held my breath. Then courage came out of nowhere and I said I want to go to bed now. I got up and ran upstairs.

Mr. Berger, Lindsey's father, exposed himself to me several times. I remember one night, we were outside and he came up behind me, rubbing his erection on my back. I cringed in fear and ran away. Several times, he exposed me to pornography. One time he told me to go up the stairs into the library and get him a book. There laid an open book of a couple engaging in intercourse. I didn't know what sex was and wasn't able to process this. Pornographic magazines were a favorite of his and I was exposed to some of these as well.

This went on for several years, until one day, I suddenly stopped going there. I can't remember what I was thinking as a child but I knew that this wasn't normal and was not safe. Lindsey changed and started acting out. Reflecting back, I believe he molested her, too.

I remember when I suddenly ended my relationship with them and my mother asked me why. And both Mrs. Berger and Lindsey kept saying, "Why aren't you coming down here anymore? We miss you." I couldn't talk about it as shame was embedded in me.

That dark secret was something I kept inside for a long time . . . until I turned 50.

Shame had a profound effect on me, although I was not aware of the extent until I entered the desert with Jesus on my deeper journey. I will share more with you in the chapters to come. I have been a Christ follower all of my life. I knew in my head God loved me but didn't really fully believe in my heart that I am His beloved daughter.

Then I went into my desert and met with Him there, waiting for me with open, accepting, loving, gentle arms. He is waiting for you, too.

Experiencing Being the Beloved

Before I could enter into a deeper relationship of healing with God, I needed to embrace in my heart how much He truly does love me. It's difficult for me to trust someone when I don't think they care about me or if I fear rejection from them. I had a hard time trusting God, wondering why this happened to me. Over time, with various spiritual practices, I am able to trust Him more.

One of these spiritual practices is Imaginative Prayer. It is simply imagining myself in the scripture and allowing God to speak to me. This practice allows one to *experience* God, in a deeper, personal way. It is not about obtaining more knowledge, although you may learn some new facts. Imaginative prayer is more about "being" with God. *Be still and know that I am God* (Psalm 46:10).

On the next page, I will describe Imaginative Prayer and then introduce one of my favorite women in scripture: the woman at the well (John 4). Women were considered property during the time of Jesus. They did not have the rights and choices we have today. They were not given an education. And yet Jesus reached out to them. He treated them as human beings, giving them value and worth. Why? Because God created men and women in His image and He loved them. Jesus didn't care what others thought of Him when he talked to a Samaritan, or that she was labeled a sinful woman. In that time, Jews despised Samaritans and would not speak to them. Jesus reached out to many women with love and compassion, offering eternal life, healing and relationship. He often reached out to those who were outcasts in society. He didn't shun them or criticize them. Instead He offered them healing, redemption and most of all love.

Just as long ago He was there for them, He is here for us today.

Imaginative Prayer

St. Ignatius of Loyola (1491-1556)[1] wrote of using our imagination in praying with the scriptures. This prayer practice is about putting yourself into a scripture passage. It can be very insightful and encouraging. You can refer to this explanation each time imaginative prayer is suggested in this material. This how I practice imaginative prayer.

Read a scripture story/passage **slowly** several times. Try not to rush through it. You may want to read it out loud if hearing the word is more helpful. Then, review it with the following questions. It might also help to close your eyes. Allow at least 10-15 min. to do this prayer.

- Describe the setting. Describe the characters.
- What is happening?
- What do you see? Hear? Taste? Touch? Smell?
- What are you feeling as the observer?
- How does this event or these characters relate to your life?
- What is God inviting you into?
- How does it make you feel towards God/Jesus?

Now put yourself into the passage. You are the main character. God/Jesus turns to you and looks at you with love in His eyes.

- What is happening?
- What do you see? Hear? Taste? Touch? Smell?
- What is God saying to you?
- Is there an invitation?
- How does this make you feel about Him?
- What is He feeling towards you?
- How does this make you feel about yourself?

Sit with God in this passage. Ask for wisdom and insight as to what this means for you.

Imaginative Prayer on the Woman at the Well

On the next few pages is an imaginative prayer exercise on the woman at the well, as told in scripture (John 4:4-26). This passage truly speaks to me and she is one of my favorites. I love how Jesus went out of His way to talk to her through the desert hills of Samaria. I saw these hills when I went to Israel. Jesus could have walked to Jerusalem by the cool waters of the Jordan River. But He had something else in mind. He didn't worry about what others thought when he talked to the sinful Samaritan woman. And once she experienced His loving transformation, her shame melted away and she was excited to share her story of healing with others. She was so filled with joy that she left something very valuable behind: her water jug. It would be like me leaving my purse or my iPhone there. Although my healing has taken some time, I am ready, like the Samaritan woman, to share my story with others so they can experience the Living Water as I have.

Read the story slowly from **John 4:4-26** in the box on the next page. Spend some time gazing at the print of Jesus and the Samaritan woman on the next page. Then read the story I have adapted entitled *The Woman at the Well: "My Story."* Following that are directions for the imaginative prayer exercise and suggested questions for reflection.

Angelica Kauffmann (1741-1807), Christ and the Samaritan Woman at the Well. 1796.

Now He had to go through Samaria. So he came to a town in Samaria called Sychar, near the plot of ground Jacob had given to his son Joseph. Jacob's well was there and Jesus, tired as he was from the journey, sat down by the well. It was about the sixth hour. When a Samaritan woman came to draw water, Jesus said to her, "Will you give me a drink?" (His disciples had gone into the town to buy food). The Samaritan woman said to him, "You are a Jew and I am a Samaritan woman. How can you ask me for a drink?" (For Jews do not associate with Samaritans).

Jesus answered her, "If you knew the gift of God and who it is that asks you for a drink, you would have asked him and he would have given you living water." "Sir," the woman said, "you have nothing to draw with and well is deep. Where can you get this living water? Are you greater than our father Jacob, who gave us the well and drank from it himself, as did also his sons and his flocks and herds?"

Jesus answered, "Everyone who drinks this water will be thirsty again, but whoever drinks the water I give him will never thirst. Indeed, the water I give him will become in him a spring of water welling up to eternal life." The woman said to him, "Sir, give me this water so that I won't get thirsty and have to keep coming here to draw water." He told her, "Go, call your husband and come back." "I have no husband," she replied. Jesus said to her, "You are right when you say you have no husband. The fact is, you have had five husbands, and the man you now have is not your husband. What you have just said is quite true."

"Sir," the woman said, "I can see that you are a prophet. Our fathers worshipped on this mountain, but you Jews claim that the place where we must worship is in Jerusalem." Jesus declared, "Believe me, woman, a time is coming when you will worship the Father neither on this mountain nor in Jerusalem. You Samaritans worship what you do not know, we worship what we do know, for salvation is from the Jews. Yet a time is coming and has now come when the true worshippers will worship the Father in spirit and truth, for they are the kind of worshippers the Father seeks. God is spirit, and his worshippers must worship in spirit and in truth."

The woman said, "I know the Messiah (called Christ) is coming. When he comes, he will explain everything to us." Then Jesus declared, "I who speak to you am He."

John 4:4-26 (NIV)

The Woman at the Well

I was an outcast in my village in Samaria. I had lived with several men over the years including the one I am with now. People would either sneer at me or avoid me. I felt so unworthy.

I would go to the well everyday around noon. I knew that was the hottest time of day and yet I wanted to go when no one else was there. I needed to hide my shame from others.

Until one day I met Him.

He was sitting there at the well. I did not recognize Him, although I guessed He was Jewish by His appearance. Jews do not speak to us Samaritans - they look down upon us. He certainly wouldn't speak to me, since not only am I a Samaritan; I am also a woman…a sinful woman. So I decided to go get my water and leave. Then I was shocked when He spoke to me. He asked for a drink of water. Baffled, I asked Him if He was asking me for a drink of water. Then He said something that made no sense at all; "If you knew the gift of God and who it is that asks you for a drink, you would have asked Him and He would have given you living water."

"Huh??" This made absolutely no sense to me. He must have been out in the sun too long. I didn't want to offend Him, so I pointed out to Him that the well was deep, and he had nothing to draw the water up with. I asked Him if he thought He was greater than our ancestor Jacob who gave us this well.

Then He said something else that was so strange to my ears. He said, "Everyone who drinks the water I give him will never thirst. Indeed, the water I give him will become in him a spring of water welling up to eternal life."

So I told Him to give me some of this living water so I don't have to come back to the well. He told me to go get my husband and come back. I said I wasn't married. Then He said that I spoke truth, that the man I was living with was not my husband, and that I'd had 5 husbands before him.

"Wow!" I was blown away. I thought, "He must be a prophet!" He continued on to say that the place to worship God is not what is important but to worship Him wherever I am. God wants me to love Him with my whole heart, mind, soul and strength. I told him that I knew someday the Messiah would come. Then His eyes pierced mine, with this amazing love . . . something I have never experienced before . . . and said, "I am He."

My eyes were opened. He is the Messiah! I was so excited that I raced to the town to tell the others that he was here. I didn't care what they thought of me. All that shame was gone. I even left my precious water jug behind!

Some of the people in town gave me this crazy look, like I didn't know what I was talking about. But I think they saw something different, something new in me. I told them to go see for themselves. More than a handful went to Him at the well and invited Him to stay with us in Samaria. As He spent two days with us, many believed He truly was the Messiah.

Epilogue:

Jesus went out of His way for me through the desert hills of Samaria. He did not care what others thought of Him as He spoke to me, spent time with me, and gave me salvation. He broke the rules by speaking to a Samaritan, a woman, and a woman of my kind; He did not condemn me for my past. Once I was filled with His love for me, I became free and did not care what the townspeople thought of me. I wanted them to experience this living water, too. The chains of disgrace had melted away.

I still need to drink the living water every day, just as I do regular water. I imagine being with Him at the well and soaking his love within the depths of my soul. I am filled with gratitude that His spirit lives within me. I still struggle with temptation, especially with men, yet his Spirit helps me make wise, moral choices. When I fall, he is there to help me back to the well, and to the Living Water. My story was written in His Holy Book and is still told to people this day. I am so grateful to share my story with you.

Sit quietly in the presence of God. Close your eyes. Breathe in and out slowly for two minutes. Imagine you are in this scene as the woman at the well.

What does this look like? _____

_____

_____

How are you feeling right now? Tired from drawing water? Worn out from the noon heat? Something else? _____

_____

_____

What are you thinking as you see Jesus sitting at the well looking at you?

_____

_____

Now He looks at you with this amazing gaze of love. He invites you to sit with Him. He talks about the Living Water.

What are you feeling right now?

_____

_____

He knows you have had five husbands (or whatever it is you have done). He does not condemn you. He tells you not to listen to the critics. He takes your hands and lovingly looks into your eyes. He offers forgiveness and eternal life.

What is He saying to you? _____

_____

_____

What is He offering you? _____

_____

_____

Where do you need to experience more freedom in your life? _____

_____

_____

How do you feel that Jesus has gone out of His way to come and be with you? _____

_____

What is your response?

_____

_____

Other passages that demonstrate Jesus' love for women:

The Bleeding Woman (Luke 8:40-48)
The Bent-Over Woman (Luke 13:10-13)
Mary and Martha (Luke 10:38-41, John 11:1-44)
The Woman Caught in Adultery (John 8:1-11)
The Woman who washes His feet with her Hair (Luke 7:36-50)
Mary, His Mother (Luke 1:1-56)
The Women He meets along the way to the Cross (Luke 23:27-30)
The Mother who son was Restored to Life (Luke 7:11-17)
Mary Magdalene and the Tomb (John 20:11-18)

Try Imaginative Prayer during your time alone with God with the above passages. Notice how Jesus reached out in love to these women. Many of these women were outcasts of society of the time. Woman who were engaged in sex outside of marriage were shunned and often stoned to death if it was adultery. When a woman had her menstrual period, she was considered unclean. If women (and men) had a handicap or illness they were often shunned by society. As I mentioned before, women were considered the property of their husbands. They did not have the freedoms we have today for career, education, or choosing their spouse. Their opinions were not heard by men. They did not have a voice.

Notice how Jesus treated women and how He speaks to you through these passages.

I hope you are getting started to enter into a deeper place with God. Writing and then sharing your story can be healing in and of itself. The key is to spend time with God every day. He does love you more than you know and desires to love and heal you so you can be free to be the woman He created you to be. Knowing you truly are the Beloved, deep in your heart and soul, will grow over the time spent with Him. Imaginative Prayer is one tool that can foster this loving relationship. In the next chapter, I will share more tools and stories on being the Beloved.

Imaginative Prayer Exercise on Being the Beloved

Jesus at the Baptism, image from snappygoat.com.

Slowly read the scripture passage. Imagine being there, watching Jesus being baptized. Then He asks you to come into the water and be baptized.

> At that time Jesus came from Nazareth in Galilee and was baptized by John in the Jordan. As Jesus was coming up out of the water, he saw heaven being torn open and the Spirit descending on him like a dove. And a voice came from heaven: "You are my Son, whom I love; with you I am well pleased."
>
> Mark 1:9-13 (NIV)

- What is going on around you? What do you see, hear and smell?
- What do you notice as you watch Jesus being baptized?
- What are you feeling when Jesus says it is your turn?
- How do you feel when God says, "This is my daughter with whom I am well pleased?"

Chapter Two
The Beloved

God's love is not limited like human love. He knows you deeply and accepts you just as you are. You can't earn His love as you already have it. You are created in His image. In this chapter, I will present various practices to help you experience more of His love. Let's start with reflecting and meditating on Psalm 139, which has helped me know just how much I am truly the beloved daughter of God.

Reflection on Psalm 139

Read Psalm 139 slowly a couple times. Then reflect on the following verses:

> 3: You discern my going out and my lying down; you are familiar with all my ways.
>
> 7: Where can I flee from your Presence?

God is everywhere and with you all the time. Journal some of your experiences with Him, when you were aware of His presence or love for you. _____

_____

_____

How does this make you feel about God? _____

_____

_____

Sit for a few minutes and ponder these verses:

> For you created my inmost being. You knit me together in my mother's womb. I praise you because I am fearfully and wonderfully made.
>
> Psalm 139:13-14

Name 20 characteristics about you. Write both internal characteristics and external gifts/talents.

_____   _____
_____   _____
_____   _____
_____   _____
_____   _____
_____   _____
_____   _____
_____   _____
_____   _____
_____   _____

Celebrate you! You are unique and gifted! When you start to go down that road of self-loathing and self-doubt, recall how fearfully and wonderfully made you are.

> How precious to me are your thoughts, O God! How vast is the sum of them!
> Psalm 139:17

Name 10 characteristics about God that are precious to you.

_____   _____
_____   _____
_____   _____
_____   _____
_____   _____

Sit and ponder your experiences of God. Embrace the characteristics about you. This is how God has fearfully and wonderfully created you to be. Sit and meditate on what you appreciate about God. Spend some time in gratitude and praise for who He is and who He created you to be.

> Search me, O God, and know my heart; test me and know my anxious thoughts. See if there is any offensive way in me, and lead me in the way everlasting.
> Psalm 139:23-24

A prayer that can be done in 10-15 minutes a day that will develop self-awareness and draw you closer to God is the Prayer of Examen (St. Ignatius of Loyola).[2] There are several versions, and below is one of my favorites, based on the verses above. I usually pray this in the morning, reflecting on the day before, or at night before I go to bed, thinking about that day. Try journaling these questions as you sit with God.

Prayer of Examen

1. Thank God for the gifts He gave me during this day. What was I grateful for? _____
   _____
   _____

2. Where did I feel God's presence? What drew me closer to God? And what drew me away from God? _____
   _____
   _____
   _____

3. Notice the feelings, both positive and negative I felt throughout the day. Ask God for wisdom as to what is going on deep inside of me. _____
   _____
   _____
   _____

4. Confess any sin or wrongdoing. Own my part. Is there anything I need to repair? __
   _____
   _____
   _____

5. Ask for the grace to help me choose what draws me closer to God and to do better tomorrow. _____
   _____
   _____
   _____

Examen of The Fruit of the Spirit

Jesus said He came to give us an abundant life, a full life (John 10:10). Some say He was talking of eternal life in heaven. Others believe He is talking of life here and now as well as in heaven. Jesus also tells us that He is the vine and we are the branches (John 15). If we abide with Him, we will bear fruit. This fruit is also mentioned by Paul in Galatians 5:22; *But the fruit of the Spirit is love, joy, peace, patience, kindness, goodness, gentleness and self-control.* I believe this is the abundant life; an internal way of being that is open to all.

As you pray, ask God for wisdom. Examine a fruit of the Spirit. See which one jumps out at you. Ask yourself these questions:

Where did I feel or experience _____ today?

Where did I show or display _____ today?

For example, where did I feel God's love for me today? Perhaps in a smile or a kind word from someone. Or a dog that wags his tail as you walk in the room. Or something I accomplished today. Even a simple task of praying for someone and sending a kind text can be an act of love.

What blocked me from _____ today? What was that about?

How can I be more _____ tomorrow?

For example, what blocked me being patient today? Road rage? Or something didn't go my way? Maybe slowing down and trying a few breath prayers while I am driving might help me be more patient in the car.

Take your time. You may want to go through several fruits or just reflect on one until you start to see a change in your life. The Holy Spirit within you can help you along the way.

Practicing Joy

> I tell you the truth, you will weep and mourn while the world rejoices. You will grieve, but your grief will turn to joy. A woman giving birth to a child has pain because her time has come; but when her baby is born, she forgets the anguish because of her joy that a child is born into the world. So with you: now is your time of grief, but I will see you again and you will rejoice; no one will take away your joy.
>
> John 16:20-22 (NIV)

This is a simple practice I learned from Sheryl Fleisher,[3] a spiritual director and minister. At any time, if you need to take a break from this hard work you are doing, try this practice:

- Name three things that brought you joy today or yesterday.
- Sit and relish these things.
- Invite Jesus into this place of joy with you.
- Journal your experience.

_____

_____

_____

_____

_____

_____

_____

_____

_____

_____

_____

_____

_____

_____

_____

_____

_____

_____

_____

Silent Soaking Prayer

I learned this prayer practice from my first spiritual director. It has been a powerful tool of God's healing transformation in my life. My wounds from the abuse left holes in me that I tried to fill with approval from other people or from success. Human love is needed and yet is limited. Work is necessary and life giving, but never fully satisfying. Only God's love is unlimited and fully satisfying. Sadly, I hear many people say they don't really believe in their hearts that God loves them. We learn conditional love through our family of origin and the culture we live in. The world tells us we are lovable if we are pretty, thin, rich, popular, successful, smart, have a perfect marriage, perfect kids, and so on. Shame is a barrier that keeps us from experiencing His love deep within our souls. What I have discovered is that I cannot do something to earn God's love. I already have it. His love is a gift. He loves me just as I am, just where I am at. I just need to sit silently and soak it in. The key is to not force it or try to control it. Just surrender and allow His love to flow through you. Over time, something mysterious happens and I am able to actually feel His love for me.

Silent Soaking prayer is a form of meditation and can be used during your 30-minute quiet time. Focused breathing reduces anxiety. Breathing through the nose enhances oxygen in the brain. Hospital research shows that patients who pray or have a faith in God heal more quickly and need less medication. Research has shown that brain chemistry and neuropathways change as a result of meditation. Those who meditate and practice silence experience less anxiety and less "stinking thinking" (critical voice). Silent prayer helps us center, bringing us to a deeper presence of God and who He created us to be.

> Be still and know that I am God.   Psalm 46:10 (NIV)

- Sit in a quiet place, alone, with no noise or distractions.
- Get comfortable. Breathe deeply. Relax.
- Breathe in the Holy Spirit. Breathe out anxiety and fear.
- Imagine sitting there quietly with God or Jesus. Maybe you are sitting with God the Father with His arms, maybe watching the sunset with Jesus in a beautiful place. Allow Jesus to put His arms around you, if it feels comfortable. Imagine the setting to be whatever brings you peace---desert, sea, mountains or elsewhere.
- Be silent. When thoughts intrude, put it in an imaginary cupboard and tend to it later. Focus on God, and on your deep, steady breathing.
- Sit. Be still. Soak in His love.

Meditation on Scripture Passages

As I stated earlier, neuroscience confirms the benefit of meditation. This practice is mentioned throughout scripture and ordained by God. Many scriptures tell us how much God loves us, and I have chosen some of my favorites. You may have a favorite you want to meditate on.

I like to compare meditation to sucking on a piece of dark chocolate or peppermint. One day my grandson put out his hand for some chocolate. He shoved it in his mouth, swallowed it, then quickly put out his hand with a big smile saying, "more please." I told him to slow down and suck on it, smell it and savor it! I handed him another piece.

What happens to dark chocolate or a peppermint when we slowly savor it? *It lingers.*

The same is true with the scripture.

How to Meditate:

- Find a comfortable, silent, and safe place.
- Relax your body. Breathe deeply in and out.
- Ask God to identify your core lie.
- Focus on your truth or scripture (e.g. I am God's Beloved or I am worthy).
- When thoughts enter in, *and they will,* put them in an imaginary cupboard.
- Focus again on your truth.
- Give this at least 10 minutes. Practice this daily if possible.

> Therefore, there is now no condemnation for those who are in Christ Jesus…the law of the Spirit [of Life] has set [me] free from the law of sin and death.
> Romans 8:1-2 (NIV)
>
> With the arrival of Jesus, the Messiah, that fateful dilemma is resolved. Those who enter into Christ's being-here-for-us no longer have to live under a continuous, low-lying black cloud.
> Romans 8:1 (MSG)

- As you meditate on the above, what jumps out at you?
- What does it look like for you, to feel no more condemnation? To live no longer under a black cloud?

> For I am convinced that neither death nor life, neither angels nor demons, neither the present not the future, nor any powers, neither height nor depth, nor anything else in all creation, will be able to separate us from the love of God that is in Christ Jesus our Lord.
>
> Romans 8:38-39 (NIV)
>
> None of this fazes us because Jesus loves us. I'm absolutely convinced that nothing—nothing living or dead, angelic or demonic, today or tomorrow, high or low, thinkable or unthinkable—absolutely nothing can get between us and God's love because of the way that Jesus our Master has embraced us.
>
> Romans 8:38-39 (MSG)

This is my favorite passage of how much God truly loves us.

Nothing. Absolutely nothing. Can separate us from His love.

- How does this scripture make you feel?
- What stirs inside of you as you meditate on this passage?

> God is love. Whoever lives in love lives in God, and God in Him. In this way, love is made complete among us so that we will have confidence on the Day of Judgment, because in this world we are like him. There is no fear in love. But perfect love drives out fear, because fear has to do with punishment. The one who fears is not made perfect in love. We love because He first loves us.
>
> 1 John 4: 16b-19

The disciple John walked intimately with Jesus. He states throughout his gospel that he was the disciple that Jesus loved. Some feel that he was favored and others feel that John truly grasped how loved he was by Jesus.

- What about you?
- Do you get it?

Loving Yourself

Scripture tells us the two greatest commandments are to love God and to love people as you love yourself. In our culture, we are encouraged to love ourselves too much (self-centered) or not enough (self-neglect). Some women tell me that they believe taking time out for themselves is selfish. They need to take care of everyone else's needs above their own. Pastor Mike Quinn,[4] lead pastor of Newbreak Church in San Diego, gave a beautiful sermon on loving ourselves. He used an illustration of two buckets of water and a sponge which represents us. He said when our sponge is dry, we cannot pour into others. Our sponge flourishes when filled. In order to give our time, energy and service to others, we need to take care of ourselves. Another analogy is when the flight attendant asks the parent to put on their oxygen mask first and then their child's.

I am a physical, emotional and spiritual being. I have learned to pay attention to my body, to hear what it needs. I examine my feelings to know what my emotional needs are. I know how to listen to the Holy Spirit and to my soul to know what I long for spiritually. These three aspects of ourselves overlap and intertwine with one another. It is difficult to separate them out as we are complex human beings. The key is to pay attention to your needs. Fill your sponge.

Scripture tells us we are created in His Image: physical, emotional and spiritual. Our physical body is important to take care of and to nurture. Our body is a dwelling place for the Holy Spirit. Stress has a way of entering our lives and slowly creates all kinds of physical problems. Some of the ways I take care of myself are: eating right, getting enough sleep, swimming, dancing, and having a massage. Some women I know love to do art, sew, garden and cook. These are just some of the many ways we can take of our bodies.

Being with loved ones nurtures my emotional being. Having fun together and laughing brings joy to me. Enjoying a good book or a movie can be a positive influence for me. Just sitting with God and allowing myself to share whatever I am feeling fills my sponge. He listens to me. I feel heard and understood.

I need time alone with God to nurture my soul, in prayer and various practices. If I find something not working any more, I try something new to connect with God. Being in nature also nurtures my soul. His creation is all around us, even in my backyard. I especially love the ocean as it reminds me how vast His love for me is. I respect the ocean and there is much I don't see . . . much I don't know. But I can feel the water over my body filling me with joy and pleasure as I swim. Simply gazing at the ocean brings calmness and draws me closer to God. When a day go by without spending time with Him, *I truly miss Him.*

When my sponge is filled, I am able to come alongside others as a spiritual director and leader of *Not Alone* groups. I love journeying with women who want to grow. I create the space for God to enter in and meet these women where they are at. I am also able to be present to my family and friends.

Give yourself permission to take care of yourself. You are worth it!

How do you love yourself? On the next two pages there are three circles, each representing your physical, emotional and spiritual selves. It is difficult to separate each part since all influence each other and overlap. I have included an example of my own life. I believe in my heart, God wants us to live in balance. We need to take the time to fill our sponges and re-charge our batteries. This includes changing bad habits that hurt us and draw us away from God. Sometimes we neglect ourselves in one area or all three. When we live in balance, we will experience more fruits of the spirit: joy, peace, patience, kindness, gentleness, goodness, faithfulness, self-control, and love.

- Do you believe in loving yourself? Why or why not?
- How do you relate to filling your sponge first or putting on your oxygen mask first?
- Where are you good at loving yourself? Where could you be better?
- What keeps you from loving yourself?
- What nurtures you?
- What drains you?
- How can you be more balanced? What do you need to change/add and what do you need to delete?
- What, specifically, is God inviting you into, in the area of loving yourself?

My example of loving myself:

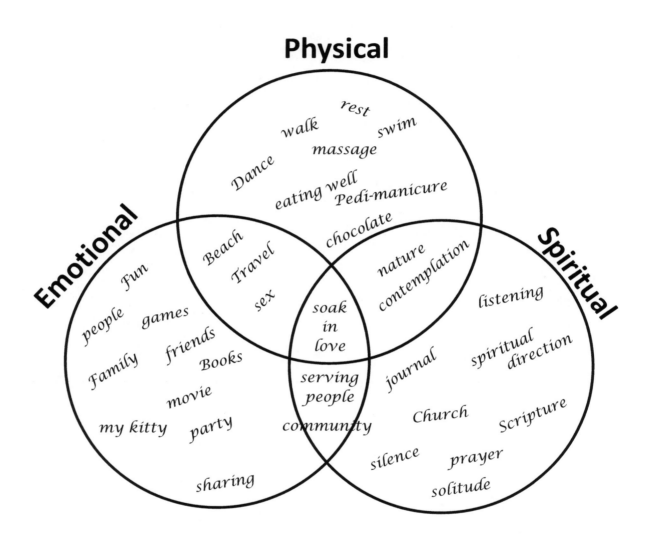

Physical

rest
walk   swim
Dance   massage
eating well   Pedi-manicure
chocolate

Emotional

Beach   Travel
Fun   sex
people   games
Family   friends   Books
movie
my kitty   party
community
sharing

nature
contemplation

soak
in
love

serving
people

Spiritual

listening
journal   spiritual direction
Church   Scripture
silence   prayer
solitude

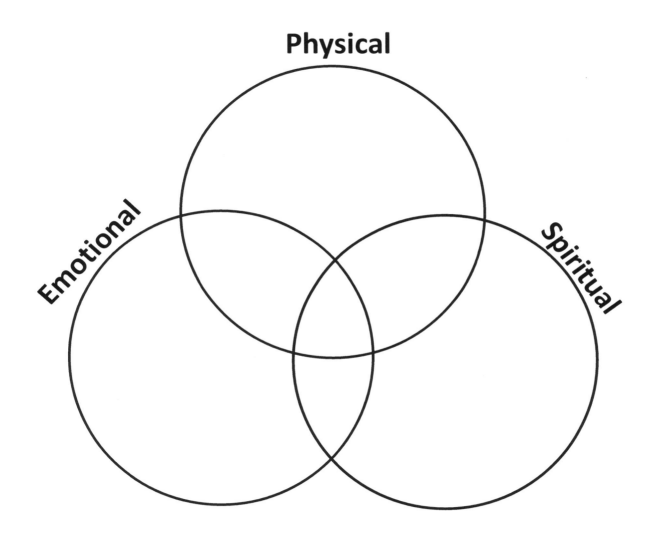

The Enemy of Self Care: "Busyness"

Busy-ness is cherished in our culture, and a part of life today. The message is to do more, to be more and to have more. More is better. Hard work is ordained by God, and He encourages us to do our best. Yet even God rested after He created the world. And He was God! Jesus modeled the balance between rest, play (wedding at Cana), and serving others as evidenced in scripture. Our culture has become out of balance with more and more emphasis on work. The problem happens when busy-ness becomes our identity. Then we have no time for God or for ourselves, leaving us drained and dry. Our human relationships can become shallow and hurried.

> As Jesus and His disciples were on their way, He came to a village; where a woman named Martha opened her home to Him. She had a sister called Mary, who sat at the Lord's feet listening to what he said. But Martha was distracted by all the preparations that had to be made. She came to Him and asked, "Lord, don't you care that my sister has left me to do the work by myself? Tell her to help me!" "Martha, Martha." the Lord answered, "you are worried and upset about many things, but only one thing is needed. Mary has chosen what is better and it will not be taken away from her."
>
> Luke 10:38-41 NIV

I think Martha gets beat up in our church sermons today. People imply that what she was doing was not worthy or not important. The passage does not imply to not be prepared for an event. And it doesn't mean that Jesus loved Mary more than Martha. He loved them both as seen in John 11. What is important is to make the right choice in the moment. Mary made the better choice in that moment.

I can be a Martha, too, with life's distractions and busy-ness. This one day, I had a powerful experience with God of making a right choice (like Mary) in the moment. I was invited to do a workshop on the Beloved Daughter of God at our church's women's retreat in Pine Valley. I had prepared and prayed over this for weeks. As I drove up there, I was feeling excited to have the opportunity. The keynote speaker started around 9:15 and I was told my workshop would be from 10:30-11:30. There were several other workshops to choose from besides mine. They gave me this lovely small chapel to do my presentation in. I arrived early enough to set up the framed picture of Jesus and the Samaritan that I brought. I wanted to share with them how Jesus went out of His way for this one woman, to offer love, redemption and living water. My materials were all ready. I sat and waited for them to arrive.

At 10:30, no women. Then 10:45 arrived. Still no women. I start to go down that road, "No one wants to hear what you have to offer. Blah…blah…blah." All of the sudden the wind came up through the pine trees., reminding me of the wind in the pines when I was a little girl with my grandma in Yosemite. All those positive memories came back to me. It was as if God was telling me to *"Stop blah blah blah. Come. Sit with me."*

I felt a peace come over me in that moment. I just sat there, listening, watching the pine trees sway in the wind. I felt His presence with me.

When 11:00 came around, there were still no women at my workshop. I am still in God's presence, feeling His love, and feeling like crying, while trying to simplify my workshop if some women come late. I don't know what is going on and I chose not to make a false assumption. I said to God that I will discern this all later but as for now, I will remain with Him. Then it was 11:15. No women.

Finally, at 11:25, one woman came up the path to the chapel. "Ok, here comes your one! I know you went out of your way for one woman, Lord, so I will do this for one woman." Then along came some more women. I was told that lunch was at 12:30 so I could have until then. My pastor's wife was at my workshop and she stated how calm I was and that I was not flustered or angry. It was because of God drawing me into His presence, through the wind in the pines, and my choice to not go down that destructive *blah blah blah* road.

You wonder what happened? I found out the keynote speaker was long-winded. She talked way over the time allowed. It had nothing to do with me. I am so grateful I didn't waste all that energy on something that wasn't true. This experience with God has helped me to stop, pay attention, and just be in the moment just as Mary did and to let go of my Martha worries.

Another powerful lesson that day for me was to let go of "the numbers game." If God brings several or even one woman to a ministry, then be content with that. Oh, yes, there is a practical side. I don't do a group or workshop if enough do not sign up to make it worth our time. However, our culture bases success on attendance. Jesus does not. I didn't hear Him say the best time was when He fed the 5,000. He was content with preaching to the multitudes or sharing hope with one Samaritan woman. Like the Apostle Paul, I have learned to be content with many or few.

Although I went that day thinking God wanted me to share with women how much He loves them, now I know He wanted to show me how much He loves me, too.

Reflection on Mary and Martha

We have both a Mary and a Martha in us. Martha represents being too busy externally or with daily task. Mary represents internal awareness of when to stop and pay attention to God. Let's first look at Martha. I do admit that there are stages in life that are busier than others. I am talking more of the "NEED" to be busy. Look at the list of common beliefs and symptoms of busy-ness.

Some common internal beliefs:

I am more valuable, worthy, respected, significant, lovable IF I have more money, bigger house, perfect children, perfect body, immaculate house, better car, biggest ministry, etc.

God loves me more when I am busy for Him.

God needs me (The Messiah Complex). Nobody can do what I do.

Resting or relaxing is being lazy.

I have to please others, so I have to say yes to them.

I SHOULD be doing this or doing that. (God does not "should" us).

Taking care of myself is selfish.

I am afraid of being alone.

Some common symptoms of being too busy:

Extreme tiredness

Lack of joy in serving God

Lack of energy in daily activities

Feelings of anxiety, especially in your body

No time for rest or self-care

Lacking joy and intimacy in your relationship with God and with others.

What do you identify with? Is it something not on this list? _____
_____

_____

Sit with God. Tell Him about your beliefs and symptoms of busy-ness. Listen. What is He saying to you?

What can you let go of so you can spend more time with God? _____
_____

Now let's look at Mary. She was able to make a better choice in the moment. I haven't always done this well but I did choose to pay attention to God that day in Pine Valley. I felt His love in wind blowing through the pine trees. I chose not to listen to my critic voice: *blah blah blah*. I reflect back on this experience when my critic voice tries to distract me away from God, away from my peace, my core of being the Beloved. I also believe in the demonic who can tempt me or get me to believe a lie. I will talk some more about the lies we believe about ourselves in Chapter Four.

What is your *blah blah blah?* Or those false assumptions you make? _____
_____
_____

Like me and the pine trees, can you reflect on a time when God showed up? _____
_____
_____

How can you pay attention to God's presence? Especially during a difficult moment? _____
_____
_____

Like Mary, how can you spend time at Jesus feet? _____
_____
_____

How do you feel that God loves both the Mary and Martha in you?
_____
_____

Spend some time with Jesus, whether you are at his feet like Mary or sitting amongst the pine trees as I did. Listen. Feel His love.

Discernment

We are presented with choices all the time. Both internal--what we are thinking, and external--what we are doing. We know right from wrong and are able to make a clear choice. Yet most of the time we face two good choices. Now this is harder to decide. For example, I hear women say they want to serve God, especially at church, but not sure which ministry to choose. Sometimes they choose what the leaders want, not what they really want. I have fallen into the trap of people pleasing and end up doing something I really don't enjoy. Now I have learned how to make the best choice, which is what God wills, and what is the desire of my heart.

Various excellent discernment exercises have been used by different spiritual directors and teachers. Some were inspired by the writings of St. Ignatius. You can use ideas like the below, or adapt your own practice.

- Begin by praying and asking God, "What is your will for me?" Then, apply what Jesus prayed in the garden, "Not my will, but thine." Relax, listen, feel His presence.

- Write down your thoughts as they come. Pray for wisdom as you ask God to guide you in making a decision.

- Make a list of the pros and cons. As you pray about your choices, imagine doing each and notice your feelings. Which choice makes you feel closer to God. If it is fear, what are you really afraid of? Is it joy, peace, or hope? Contentment? Write down your feelings.

- Confide in a trusted friend or mentor and ask for their counsel.

- After you have made a choice, wait awhile, several days if possible, and notice if the peace, joy, etc. remains. If you feel upset, anxious, discontent, then try to discern some more about what is causing this. St. Ignatius wrote about distinguishing between an angel of darkness and an angel of light. Sometimes the evil one disguises himself as an angel of light to confuse us and have us choose the least choice, not the best.

- We also can choose what to dwell on in our heads, what thoughts we entertain or make false assumptions. Write some of these thoughts down. Ask yourself if this is true? Ask God if there is something you need insight or healing on. Do these thoughts draw me closer or away from God? If your thoughts are not true and possibly causing you harm, then take these captive to Christ (2 Cor 10:5).

One of my favorite books on discernment is written by Timothy Gallagher: *Discerning God's Will: An Ignatian Guide to Christian Decision Making.*[5] Another book to help with discerning voices was written by Neil Anderson: *Victory over the Darkness.*[6]

The Role Model of Jesus

Jesus knew He was the Beloved of God. During His own baptism (Mark 1:9-11) and the Transfiguration (Matt. 17:1-13), God said that He was His beloved son with whom He was well pleased. Jesus' identity and sense of value, significance and worth were grounded in knowing and being that He was the beloved son of God.

Jesus was able to discern God's voice throughout His ministry, including from the enemy as seen in the desert (Matt. 4:1-11). He boldly stood up to Satan, grounded in His identity, and resisted temptation. He knew His call and what God wanted Him to do.

From that place of being the Beloved, Jesus looked at those He healed with loving compassion. He gazed into the leper's eyes and lovingly said, "I want to heal you." (Matt. 8:1). He didn't care that lepers were outcasts in society.

Jesus ignored those who looked down upon the Samaritan woman, the bleeding woman, the woman who washed His feet with her hair, and the woman caught in adultery. He was free from caring what other people thought of Him. He elevated women. He often went out of His way for them, because He loved them (John 4, Luke 8:30-48, Luke 7:36-60, John 8:1-11).

Jesus stood up to the religious leaders of the time, the Pharisees who criticized Him for doing good deeds on the Sabbath. In those days, no work of any kind was done on the Sabbath. They were more concerned about preserving their status, rules, and theology than God. Jesus broke the rules by healing people, including a man with a shriveled hand, on the Sabbath (Mark 3:1-6).

Jesus also loved Himself as he took care of His needs.

He retreated (Mark 1:35).

He took naps (Luke 8:23).

He went to dinner parties. Some were at the homes of Zacchaeus, Levi (Mark 2:15), Nicodemus (John 3), Mary and Martha (Luke 10:38-41).

He had fun and went to celebrations such as the wedding at Cana (John 2:1-11).

He graciously received a very expensive pedicure. Mary, from Bethany, washed his feet with perfume in an alabaster jar (Matt. 26:6-13).

In summary, you truly are the beloved daughter of God, fearfully and wonderfully made with gifts and talents for a purpose. Rejoice in God and how He has carefully knit you together. Embrace who you are. Celebrate, as there is only one you! Love yourself. Take care of yourself. Then you are giving and serving can flow out of that place of fullness, out of that place of love.

Pay attention to busy-ness, not the kind that is necessary for everyday life, but the kind that draws you away from God or leaves you feeling depleted. Notice those worrisome videos that play in your head. Try not to go down that *blah blah blah* road. Discern when God is calling you to Him and what He is asking of you. Give yourself some grace. All this takes time to re-wire your brain and make the best choices.

Notice His presence throughout your day as He is with you always. Look for ways to spend some time with the One who loves you far more than you know. He is waiting for you.

In the next chapter, I will discuss exploring one's Image of God and how a faulty image can block us from being the Beloved. Learning how to trust God is crucial to experience deeper intimacy with Him.

Chapter Three
Trusting God

My psychologist told me I had trust issues, especially with those in authority. She told me that I struggled with trusting my own intuition. I even struggled with trusting God. I remember a light bulb went on inside me.

I grew up Catholic and attended Catholic school until 8th grade. My experience of school was very positive. *Although I didn't have any inappropriate interactions with clergy, I express great sadness for those of you who did.* Whether the abuser is clergy, teacher, relative, parent, sibling, neighbor; it causes harm and creates trust issues. God is angry when people are abused. Jesus grieves over those who have been harmed in this way. I don't know why He allowed it or didn't stop it from happening to me. What I do know is that I have grown through my brokenness. I am now able to journey with those whose hearts have been broken. I am confident that in time, your trust and joy can be restored to you as well.

Trauma creates trust issues. Someone, usually older and stronger, violated this weaker individual in some way. This often leads to mistrusting people, especially authority figures. In addition, these feelings of mistrust along with our other experiences with authority figures are sometimes projected onto God. Many people are not aware of how these projections affect their relationship with God. Exploring our false images of God is crucial in order to build a loving, safe and trusted relationship with Him.

Trust is earned, and trust takes time. This is so true of our human relationships. God is not human and is faithful to His character and promises. As I have spent time with God and experienced Him, I know He is trustworthy. Many women ask me why such a loving, trustworthy God allowed this suffering to happen to them and to others. I do not have an answer for that. I do know He sees and cares what happens to us. Let's look at the story of Tamar from scripture and then the story of my friend, Maddison.

The Story of Tamar

In the course of time, Amnon, son of David fell in love with Tamar, the beautiful sister of Absalom, son of David. Amnon became frustrated to the point of illness on account of his sister Tamar, for she was a virgin, and it seemed impossible for him to do anything to her. Now Amnon had a friend named Jonadab son of Shimeah, David's brother. Jonadab was a very shrewd man. He asked Amnon, "Why do you, the king's son, look so haggard morning after morning? Won't you tell me?" Amnon said to him, "I'm in love with Tamar, my brother Absalom's sister." "Go to bed and pretend to be ill," Jonadab said. "When your father comes to see you, say to him, I would like my sister Tamar to come and give me something to eat. Let her prepare the food in my sight so I may watch her and then eat it from her hand."

So Amnon lay down and pretended to be ill. When the king came to see him Amnon said to him, "I would like my sister Tamar to come and make some special bread in my sight, so I may eat from her hand. David sent word to Tamar at the palace: "Go to the house of your brother Amnon and prepare some food for him." So Tamar went to the house of her brother Amnon, who was lying down. She took some dough, kneaded it, made the bread in his sight and baked it. Then she took the pan and served him the bread, but he refused to eat.

"Send everyone out of here," Amnon said. So everyone left him. Then Amnon said to Tamar, "Bring the food here into my bedroom so I may eat from your hand." And Tamar took the bread she had prepared and brought it to her brother Amnon in his bedroom. But when she took it to him to eat, he grabbed her and said, "Come to bed with me, my sister." "Don't my brother!" she said to him. "Don't force me. Such a thing should not be done in Israel! Don't do this wicked thing. What about me? Where could I get rid of my disgrace? And what about you? You would be like one of the wicked fools in Israel. Please speak to the king; he will not keep me from being married to you." But he refused to listen to her, and since he was stronger than she, he raped her.

Then Amnon hated her with intense hatred. In fact, he hated her more than he had loved her. Amnon said to her, "Get up and get out!" "No!" she said to him. "Sending me away would be a greater wrong than what you have already to done to me." But he refused to listen to her. He called his personal servant and said, "Get this woman out of here and bolt the door after her." So, his servant put her out and bolted the door after her. She was wearing a richly ornamented robe, for this was the kind of garment the virgin daughters of the king wore. Tamar put ashes on her head and tore the ornamented robe she was wearing. She put her hand on her head and went away, weeping aloud as she went.

Her brother, Absalom said to her, "Has that Amnon, your brother, been with you? Be quiet now, my sister, he is your brother. Don't take this thing to heart. And Tamar lived in her brother Absalom's house, a desolate woman. When King David heard all this, he was furious. Absalom never said a word to Amnon, either good or bad; he hated Amnon because he had disgraced his sister Tamar.

2 Samuel 13:1-22 (NIV)

Tamar's Story

I was the daughter of a king. My father, King David, the second king over Israel, is considered one of the great kings of all times. When he was a youth, he defeated the giant Goliath with only a sling shot. He fought many battles over the years achieving numerous victories. Many people revered my father and still do so today. And it is written that he had favor with God, since he was a man after God's heart.

Yet, he abandoned me at my greatest hour of need.

My half-brother, Amnon, was obsessed with me even though I didn't know it at the time. One day, my father told me to go prepare food for Amnon, since he was ill in bed. I went to Amnon's place and made him some bread. When it was ready, I offered the pan of bread to him but he refused to take it. He sent everyone out of the room. He then asked me to bring the bread into his bedroom so he could eat it from my hand. I felt uneasy but he is my brother and he is ill. When I approached his bed, he grabbed me and said to come to bed with him. I panicked and begged him to let me go. I pleaded with him to go to our father, King David, to allow us to marry. I did not want to live in disgrace. Yet Amnon refused to listen to me.

Then he raped me.

I was devastated, full of disgrace and misery. My soul felt so much anguish beyond words. When it was over, Amnon looked at me with hatred in his eyes. He told me to get out of his sight. I felt like he had just jabbed a sword in my stomach and then twisted it to deepen the pain. I fell on my knees, begging him not to send me away for that was even worse dishonor than what he did to me. He refused to listen to me, threw me out and bolted the door behind me.

I burst into tears. I felt so defiled, so full of shame. My heart was in a pit of despair. I tore my richly ornamented robe since I was no longer a virgin and put ashes on my head. Tears of grief were overflowing from my tormented soul.

Then Absalom, my brother, heard my crying. He suspected that Amnon had raped me. Instead of consoling me or doing something to help me, he told me to be quiet. Just keep it a family secret. Don't air the family's dirty laundry. These were the words I heard flowing from his mouth. I then went to live with Absalom as a desolate and shunned woman.

My father, David heard what happened. I said to myself, surely my father will do something. He will avenge this misdeed for me. He has fought enemies and slayed Goliath and he is a man after God's heart. I heard my father was furious at Amnon.

And yet…he did nothing.

I felt like I had a triple betrayal: first my brother, Amnon, then Absalom, and now my own father. Sometimes I feel it hurt me more that my father did nothing to help me than the actual attack. I lived the rest of my life in shame.

After some time, Absalom took justice in his own hands and killed Amnon. He rebelled against my father and was exiled. He died by the sword of one of my father's soldiers. My father grieved over his loss as he loved Absalom very much. Such tragedy in our family resulted from the outpouring of abuse.

Yet, God heard my cry. I don't know why He didn't stop it, but I know He was full of anguish over what happened to me. He put my story in His Holy Book for others to read, to know that you are not alone. I know many of you shared your abuse with your parents or other family member who did nothing to help you. Remember that God is one who sees all, He knows what happened, and vengeance is His. You don't need to live in shame as I did.

In this story, Amnon, tricked Tamar in being alone with him. He then overpowered her and raped her. She begged him to do the right thing and he refused. He used her and discarded her like a piece of trash. She felt tremendous shame as she put ashes on her head and tore her clothes. David, her father, heard of what happened. Although he was enraged, he did nothing to punish Amnon or help Tamar in her greatest hour of need.

She must have felt deep betrayal, first from her brother Amnon, then from her brother Absalom who told her to hush, and finally from her father who did not protect her or do anything to bring justice. Many women, like Tamar, have been abused by someone they trusted, often someone in the family. Many women were also betrayed by a parent who did nothing.

Amber: *It was actually worse for me that my father did nothing when I told him what the neighborhood boy said to me. I felt a double betrayal.*

Maddison: *My mother didn't believe me when I told her about my step-father. She defended him and took his side. She thought I made it all up. I felt so betrayed.*

Darla: *My family experienced the consequences of generational sin being passed down. My mother was molested by my grandfather, and yet she was the first one who had the courage to stop the abuse.*

Pamela: *He did what no father should do.*

Mariah: *I felt so betrayed by my mother. She was supposed to hear me, believe me and protect me. She did not.*

As you reflect on this story, how do you identify with Tamar? Betrayal? Shame? Keeping a secret? Parents or others who did nothing? _____

_____

_____

_____

_____

_____

_____

_____

    God saw what happened to Tamar, and I believe He was angry and grieved over it. He let us know her story by having it written in scripture. If you are a survivor of abuse, I believe He was angry and grieved over your trauma. Like Tamar, you are not alone. Talk to God, your spiritual director, or another trusted person about your feelings.

You may want to journal your feelings here.

_____

_____

_____

_____

_____

_____

_____

_____

_____

_____

_____

_____

    I have listened to many women who felt a double betrayal as Tamar did. The following is from Maddison.

Maddison's Story

I was six years old. My parents were divorced and my mom got a new boyfriend. He would have me sit on his lap. At first, it was warm and cuddling. Then one day, he put his hand down my pants and began fondling me. When I was 7, he tried to put his penis in me. This was the start of my horrible, hellish childhood.

He threatened me that if I told, he would leave my mom. I knew that would destroy her. She was a mess and so dependent on him. When I was in the 3rd grade, I couldn't stand it any longer. I told my mother. She blamed me and thought I was trying to stop her from marrying him. She accused me of lying and took me a therapist. I felt so invisible. I felt stuck and didn't want to go to therapy. I went a few times and hated it. Then I told the therapist I made the whole molestation story up. Therapy ended. And I was alone.

When I was in the 5th grade, I told him he was sick. He sobbed and sobbed and said he was molested by his baby sitter. I was so scared that I would become a molester (but I did not). When I was 16, I started ice skating. I began to sleep in my skating outfit of leotards and a body suit. I told my mom and him that I had to get up too early and didn't have time to get dressed. In reality, I was trying to find a way to protect myself. This plan did stop the night visits.

When I got a car, he had less access to me. I remember many times he tried to sweet talk me, called me beautiful and wanted to run away with me. I was just happy to have a car so I could get away from him.

I had three younger sisters in my house and I became very fearful and concerned about them. I told my father what happened to me and he was able to get custody of my sisters. He asked me if I wanted to come, too, but I said no. My abuser threatened me with lies, saying they were going to put me in jail! I was full of fear so I stayed home with my mom and him. I had my own plan to protect myself; I would skate, I had a car and a job and I would plan to get out of the house.

I realized, for the first time when I was 16 that his behavior, his so-called love for me, was so abusive. I told my boyfriend what happened to me. He was so furious and wanted to go and kill him.

Then one day, I challenged him and asked how much longer was he going to lie in front of my mother. He started sobbing. My mother couldn't deny it anymore. She threw him out. After that, she flipped out and became depressed. That's when our roles reversed and I became the parent.

I developed a shopping addiction. I would live at Nordstrom's. I filled that wound with things. Yet they never seemed to satisfy.

At 18, I was finally on my own. I went to Chuck Swindoll's church one day. I heard the message of salvation and the grace of Jesus and I was saved. This was the beginning of my journey of healing and freedom.

It took me awhile to find a good therapist that I could connect with. Once I did, I was able to work through my co-dependency of Role Reversal when I became the parent with my mother. I learned Fear Mapping, which helped me fall asleep at night. I struggled with feeling safe at night (because of his night visits) and I learned how to turn this off. I gained insight on the Pleasure Response, which is common for many survivors. Being molested is confusing as a child since our bodies are designed to respond to pleasure. I learned to separate the wrong, the abuse to my body, from its natural design to respond to pleasure, which is not wrong.

I also did a 12-step program through Adult Children of Alcoholics Anonymous. Some books that were very helpful to me during my healing process were: *Transformational Healing* by Johan and Paula Sanford, *The Healing of Damaged Emotions* by David Seemans, and *It Will Never Happen to Me* by Claudia Black.

But Jesus was the key to my healing when He called me to the serve the poor and those who were lost spiritually. This was way out of my comfort zone. I had to raise support, trust people in another culture I didn't know, and trust God. Saying yes to Jesus had a tremendous impact on my life. He asked something "big" of me. I stepped out, in faith, and went. I had the most amazing experience.

Then I knew God had my back.

Exploring Your Image of God

To trust in God, we need to explore our image of Him. Whether we are aware of it or not, almost all of us project our human authority figures onto God. If our father was strict, then God must be strict. If our mother was critical, then God is critical. In my experience as a spiritual director, I have heard people talk of not trusting God or having a block with God, especially those who have experienced abuse. One woman told me she felt God was distant because her parents were distant and unavailable.

Other important figures growing up such as clergy, teachers, grandparents, relatives, siblings also influence our image of God. We also project positive images onto God as well. If my father called me his precious daughter, then I am more able to believe that God feels this way about me, too. Sadly, mine did not. Since my father had anger issues, I felt God did, too. The molestation left me with feelings of not being valued and God didn't care what happened to me. Now I know these projections are nothing but lies. These faulty images or lies we believe about God can block us from trusting Him, from drawing close to Him, and allow His healing power in our lives. As with our human relationships, it takes time to get to know Him. He longs for a deep relationship with you.

Although I will refer to God as "He," I believe God has both male and female characteristics. Genesis 1:27 states that God made humans in His image. In Deuteronomy, God is referred to as a mother eagle. In Isaiah 66:13, God is a comforting mother. According to Wikipedia, much has been debated over the Holy Spirit referred to as both *he and she*. In scripture, the Greek work for "spirit" is *pneuma* which is not gender specific. In Genesis 1:2, the Hebrew word for "spirit" is *ruach* which is feminine. Most of the words in scripture do refer to the "spirit" as *He*. Yet God is not human.

I say these things because women who have been abused by men, especially fathers, have a hard time trusting God. Some have been able to open up when they experience God as male and female. In Paul Young's book: *The Shack,*[7] he writes a fictional story of God the Father as a woman, Jesus is male and the Holy Spirit is female. The main character, Mac, experienced horrible abuse by his father and then his daughter was murdered by a perpetrator. In the book, God so graciously appears to Mac as a woman in order to draw him into a healing relationship. God knew he wasn't ready for a father in the beginning and met him where he was at.

I believe God will meet you where you are at.

I encourage you to explore your image of God and any lies you believe about God. On the next two pages in an exercise I initially learned in my Spiritual Direction training program: Christian Formation Direction Ministries (CFDM) from the leader, Larry Warner.[8] He is a spiritual director, minister and the founder of *b*-ministries. This exercise explores my image of God--not the image in my head but the one I really felt in my heart and couldn't admit it. I have adapted this exercise and included projections, both positive and negative, from women I have journeyed with. Read over each one and see if you can identify.

ANGRY	*My father was an angry man.*
STRICT	*I learned God was about obeying rules. If I broke them, I was punished.*
FEARFUL	*The molestation created fear for me.*
TOO BUSY	*Does He really care about little old me? God is too busy for me.*
DOESN'T LISTEN	*I didn't feel heard as a child.*
DOESN'T VALUE ME	*It is my entire fault.*
NOT MY PROTECTOR	*Where was He when I was being abused?*
NOT CARING	*He is withholding good blessings from me.*
IS FEMALE, TOO	*My mother was the spiritual leader and she was caring.*
ENCOURAGER	*My grandmother loved God and was encouraging to me.*
LOVING	*There were people in my life who were Christians and loved me.*
ACCEPTING	*I had a positive experience in Catholic School growing up.*
DEMANDING	*I must work hard to earn God's love.*
DISTANT	*My parents were not around; they were not present to me.*
PERFECTIONIST	*I had to be perfect and earn good grades to be loved.*
CONTROLLING	*I had to be in control because if I expressed my anger, I lost.*
HARSH	*My father was harsh.*
CRITICAL	*My mother was critical.*

Ask God for wisdom and ponder these questions:

What did I learn about God growing up? From my family of origin? Clergy? Teachers? Church? Others? _____

_____

_____

_____

_____

What has happened in my life that has caused me to doubt or not believe in my heart that God really loves me? Or that God is really there for me? _____

_____

_____

_____

_____

_____

What happened in my life that showed me God truly loves me and was there for me? _____

_____

_____

_____

_____

_____

What do I project onto God? What do I really believe about Him but am afraid to admit? (Its ok…He does not judge you). _____

_____

_____

_____

_____

_____

Once you have identified any false projections, can begin to replace these with truth. Although there is so much to say about who God is, I will share some truths and promises that have helped me trust Him. In your quiet time, meditate on these truths.

Meditation on Truth of God

- God is good.
- God is the Creator. What He made was good (Gen. 1:31). And so beautiful!
- God is gracious and compassionate, slow to anger, abounding in love (Ps. 145:8).
- God is infinite and beyond my understanding and yet I can have a relationship with Him (Gen. 1:27, Isaiah 55:8-9).
- God created me in His image. I am fearfully and wonderfully made (Ps. 139:13-14).
- God's spirit is in me, guiding, comforting, helping me. I am not alone (John 12:27, 12-15).
- Nothing can separate me from His love. **Not a thing** (Romans 8:38-39).
- He is for me, not against me. God has my back (Romans 8:31).
- All things work together for good, even the hard times in life. (Romans 8:28).
- God loves me more than I know (John 3:16).
- God is Audient: one who hears. And He genuinely wants to listen to me (Ex. 2:23-25 MSG, 3:7 NIV).
- I am His beloved with whom He is well pleased. I don't have to earn His approval, love and respect. I already have it (Matt. 3:17, 1 John 3:1).
- God is my emotional Healer, Jehovah Rapha (Ex.15-16).
- God is wise and gives me wisdom (James 1:5).
- God is love (1 John 4:16).
- God is my strength, gives me courage and is with me wherever I go (Joshua 1:9).

What are some truths you know about God?

_____

_____

_____

_____

_____

_____

_____

_____

_____

_____

_____

Lectio Divina

Many women ask me, "Why does God allow this to happen to me?" "Why didn't He stop it?" "Does He really care, really see what happened to me?" "Why must I/he/she suffer?"

Amber: *Part of my healing was knowing that Jesus was there, in the corner, with tears in his eyes. He was angry at what was happening to me. "El Roi" is "My God who sees." That brings comfort to my soul. He really cared about what happened to me.*

Although I do not know why bad things happen to good people, I do know that God did see what happened to you. He was there. And He was angry at those who caused harm to you and was mourning over what happened to you. We live in a broken world. Evil exists. We all have free will to make choices. Sometimes we are affected by another's harmful, sinful choices. Sometimes we are in the wrong place at the wrong time. I may not fully understand until I am in heaven. I do believe that we do not see the big, finished picture. When I reflect back on my own suffering, I can see how I survived and how God was with me, even though He didn't stop it. I have grown through all this pain. He is able to use my wounds, my experiences of God and my healing to help others.

Lectio Divina is simply reading scripture out loud, allowing God to speak to our soul. Some people, especially those who are auditory processors, benefit from listening to the scripture. Dr. Christine Paintner [9] describes in her book; *Lectio Divina the Sacred Art* four movements in this prayer practice.

The passage is read slowly three times.

1. **Listen for a word or phrase that jumps** out at you. She compares this to chewing a piece of food.
2. **Reflect** on any images, feelings, memories that stir inside you. She relates this to savoring on the piece of food.
3. **Listen for an invitation** from God. Is He asking something of me? This can be compared to digesting the food.
4. **Slow down and be still** in God's presence. This is more about being with God, not doing for God. I think of this as the satisfying feeling and resting after a big thanksgiving dinner.

Try Lectio Divina with the passage on the next passage. Follow the steps above. If you are in a group, the leader may choose to read the passage. One woman found it helpful to record herself and then listen to it when she was alone.

The God Who Sees; The God Who Mourns

During that long period, the king of Egypt died. The Israelites groaned in their slavery and cried out, and their cry for help because of their slavery went up to God. God heard their groaning and He remembered His covenant with Abraham, with Isaac and with Jacob. So God looked on the Israelites and was concerned about them.

Exodus 2:23-25 (NIV)

Many years later the king of Egypt died. The Israelites groaned under their slavery and cried out. Their cries for relief from their hard labor ascended to God:

God listened to their groaning

God remembered His covenant with Abraham, with Isaac, and with Jacob

God saw what was going on with Israel

God was concerned

Exodus 2:23-25 (MSG)

The Lord said, "I have indeed seen the misery of my people in Egypt, I have heard them crying out because of their slave drivers and *I am concerned about their suffering.*"

Exodus 3:7 (NIV)

What word or phrase jumps out at you? _____
_____
_____

What does this mean to you? _____
_____
_____

What are you mourning over? _____
_____
_____

How does this make you feel that God is concerned about you?
_____
_____

The Wailing Wall in Jerusalem
Photograph by Katie Richardson, 2014, used with permission.

Here is a picture of the Wailing Wall in Jerusalem. People come to weep and pour out their prayer requests to God. They write them on a paper and place it in the crevices.

- What are you mourning over?

- What do you really, really want God to do for you?

- What is written on your piece of paper?

The Our Father

Matthew 6:9-13

Our Father in heaven
Hallowed be thy name
Your kingdom come
Your will be done
On earth as it is in heaven
Give us today our daily bread
Forgive us our debts as we also forgive our debtors
And lead us not into temptation
But deliver us from the evil one

Our Father who art in heaven, hallowed be thy name

Express praise and gratitude to God for who He is. _____.

Your kingdom come, Your will be done on earth as it is in heaven.

What is your will for me today, God? _____.

Give us this day our daily bread.

Pray for others and for myself. What do I/we need for today? _____.

Forgive us our debts as we also forgive our debtors.

Forgive me for_____. Forgive _____for _____.

And lead us not into temptation.

Help me not be tempted by _____.

But deliver us from the evil one.

Protect me from the evil one_____.

Practicing His Presence

Not only can you have time with God in your silent, sacred space, you also can experience His presence throughout the day. Brother Lawrence wrote a book called *The Practice of the Presence of God*. He was a monk and a cook for the monastery. He stated that we can practice God's presence throughout our day even in mundane tasks like cooking. For example, cooking involves putting ingredients together to make a meal. One can pray and reflect while cooking, asking God what new ingredients would He like to add to my life? Is there something He would like to create in me? Where can I be more creative in my life?

Look at your day. Ask yourself: How can I experience God in _____?

Here are some practical suggestions:

- When taking a shower, imagine God loving you as the warm water flows over your body.
- When you are holding a baby and the baby smiles at you, feel the pleasure as if God is smiling at you with love.
- When you exercise, try to pray during that time instead of using an iPod.
- When you do laundry, ask if there is something internal that needs to be clean? (negative thinking, criticism, bitterness, regrets, etc.)
- As you watch the sunrise, ask God what is something new to begin my day?
- As you watch the sunset, ask God what do you need to let go of today?
- As you pet your dog or cat, what do you learn about God or others through animals?
- When you are driving, try turning off the radio and use this time for prayer.
- Use art as a way to connect with God.
- **Stop and Pay Attention to God's Presence.** (The wind in the pine trees, Chap.2).
- As you get out in nature, be still and let God talk to you. God created the world and all its beauty for us to enjoy. Seeing the majestic mountains in Yosemite or the barren desert in Palm Springs, connects me with God. I feel a sense of awe and wonder. One of my favorite places in nature is the ocean. On the next page is a practice you can try.

Practicing God's Presence in Nature

The Eiger, Mönch, and Jungfrau mountains in Switzerland. *Photo by Ron Richardson, used by permission.*

Here are some questions to ponder as you go out in nature. This is God's creation, His artwork, His gift to us.

- As you sit quietly in nature, what do you notice? Use your five senses.
- What are the characteristics you enjoy about_____? (ocean, park, desert).
- How do these characteristics relate to God?
- How does God reveal Himself to you through the _____?
- How does being here at the _____ make you feel?
- What is God inviting you into?

Trusting God: The Model of Jesus and Thomas

Jesus modeled trust in God throughout His ministry. He trusted God when the spirit led Him into the desert to be tempted (Matt. 4:1). He believed God would take care of Him and would give Him a tool (scripture) to handle temptation.

Jesus often retreated alone to be with God and to pray. He trusted God that His will would be done (Mark 1:35).

Although He asked God to take away the cup (salvation through the cross), He surrendered His will to God and trusted Him with the outcome (Matt. 26:34).

You may be thinking that Jesus is fully God and fully human, so of course He trusted God. He knew what would happen. Then I encourage you to look at Thomas, one of His disciples.

Thomas walked with Jesus, he witnessed His miracles, he heard His preaching and experienced His love. When Jesus was crucified, he fled in fear with the other apostles to hide. After the resurrection, Thomas told the others he would not believe Jesus rose from the dead unless he put his hands in His wounds. He doubted Jesus arose as He said He would. And yet Jesus was compassionate to Thomas when He appeared to him (John 20:27). He did not criticize him for doubting. He did not beat him up for abandoning him at the cross. Instead, He offered Thomas to put his hands in His side and touch the wounds in His hands. What an amazing gesture of love and grace! Thomas' faith and trust were deepened as a result.

I believe it is ok if you doubt. We all struggle with doubt and trust in God at times. When in doubt, go to Jesus. He won't criticize you. He was open to Thomas and He will be open to you. Jesus said *blessed are those who believe who have not seen.* And that is you and me!

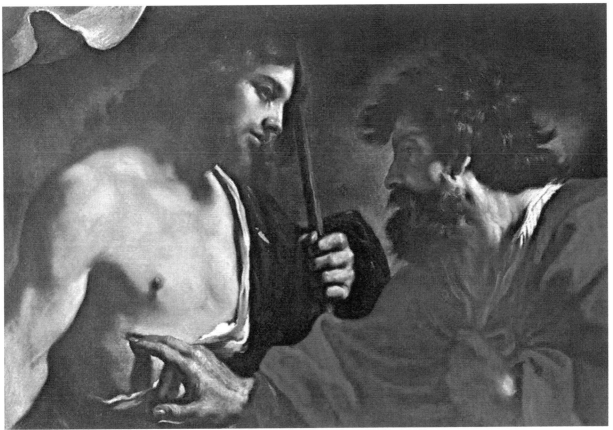

Doubting Thomas by Guercino (1591-1666)
Oil on canvas, Residenzgalerie, Salzburg, Austria

- Notice the look of love on Jesus' face as He gazes at Thomas.
- Imagine Jesus looking at you in the same way He does Thomas.
- How does that make you feel?
- What do you doubt?
- What does He offer you?

Here is a practice that I do every day called TRUST.

Spiritual Practice: TRUST

<u>T</u>: Time

- The key is to spend time alone with God. This is intentional time. Like having a date night or quality time with a loved one. In the first chapter, we talked about creating a sacred space. In addition to intentional time, you can practice His presence throughout your day.

<u>R</u>: Reflect

- I reflect on my day with Prayer of Examen (St. Ignatius of Loyola, Chapter Two).

<u>U</u>: Unload

- Lament if I need to. David lamented in the Psalms and He was a man after God's heart. If He can lament, so can I and so can you.
- Ask for my needs and pray for others.

<u>S</u>: Silence

- After me doing the talking, it is time for me to listen to Him.
- Some of the practices that have been transforming for me are Soaking in His Love, Meditation, Centering Prayer and Being Still: simply listening to His voice.

<u>T</u>: Thanksgiving

Neuroscience confirms the positive benefits of practicing gratitude on the brain. God talks about it throughout His Word! Gratitude helps us experience contentment and a sense of joy. Sometimes I begin my time in prayer with thanksgiving and then end with gratitude.

- Express to God what you were thankful or grateful for the day. Name both the small and the large gifts received. Sit for a while and allow gratitude to fill your heart.

God is a mystery (Eph. 3:9). He is known and yet unknown. We can get to know Him through the Bible and nature that He created for us. God is good. God is love. We see His character in Jesus, who is God in flesh. We see how Jesus went out of His way to love others, especially these women in scripture who did not feel love or value in this life. The same is true for us today. Discover any lies you believe about Him and replace it with the truth. Its ok if you doubt sometimes. He is there waiting for you with open arms. Jesus has wounds, He understands yours. His love is extravagant, unmeasurable, without end and He longs to draw you into His friendship. Spend time with Him. Get to know Him. Allow His love and healing flow through you to become the woman you were created to be; beautiful, valued and with a purpose.

Not only do faulty images about God hold us back from love, healing and transformation but so do the lies that we believe about ourselves. We will discuss shame in the next chapter.

Chapter Four
Shame and Unworthiness

I couldn't tell my parents or anyone for years. It was my secret. Later I felt shame for not telling on him. Maybe I could have stopped him. I carried that burden of guilt for not reporting him. I also felt shame for what he did to me, as if it was my fault. In reality, I had been living in a Hansel and Gretel story. I had wanted the fun, the cake, and the goodies, and just hoped I could avoid the evil witch.

Shame is like a cancer. It destroys the good cells and eats away at the organs that are necessary for life. Shame robs us of our worth as the beloved, and our intimate relationship with God. It lies deep within, permeating our whole being. That is why I was devastated when someone I thought was my friend called me after my 50th birthday party and attacked my integrity as a leader. Although this was not her intention, I perceived this as her shaming me. She tapped into that deep wound. Now I can reflect back, I see how I overreacted. The disagreement was over a difference of opinions and beliefs. However, God had another plan. He wanted to take that wound, clean out the pus, and give it His medicine so I could heal. Like most people, I was not aware of my shame. It was too painful to admit.

Most children who have been abused experience shame. Even adults who have been abused by another adult feel a sense of unworthiness, that somehow, they deserved it. Children blame themselves for the abuse. Common beliefs are: "It was my fault," "I must have done something wrong," or "I deserved it."

Amber: *I felt I deserved it because I was wearing a gypsy costume for Halloween.*

Some women, like me, felt shame because they didn't tell anyone.

Some women felt shame because they did tell their parents, but they did nothing about it. It was a double betrayal, first from the abuser and then from the parents who didn't protect them.

Amber: *I felt unworthy because my dad did nothing to help me.*

Pamela: *I felt unworthy because my father did what no father should do.*

Maddison: *I told my mother and she said it was my fault. She thought I was making it up.*

Mariah: *I was so angry at my mother, who did nothing when I told her what he did.*

In this chapter, we will share our shame with each other. Admitting shame is for your benefit allowing a powerful bondage to be broken. The "secret" loses its power over us and we can begin to heal. I will discuss the difference between healthy conviction and unhealthy or toxic shame. We will look at the story of the bleeding woman, who lived in shame, in Luke 8:30-48. And then I would like to share my friend Amber's story with you.

iStock photo

- As you gaze at this picture, what do you notice?
- How do you relate to her?

There was a guy who lived next door.

He was actually a young man, between 18 and 19 years old. I was 10 years old. It happened around Halloween. I was dressed in a gypsy costume. He told me his dog died and asked me if I wanted to see the bones. I said yes and followed him into the garage. He told me to pull up my skirt. Before I knew it, my pants were down and he was rubbing his penis against me. I was so frightened.

I remember going home and I told my parents. My father just laid in bed and did nothing. My mother went over and confronted his mother who became hysterical. She said that her Junior would never do anything like that, and I was the one who was wrong. My parents never did anything more. He didn't try to approach me after that and then he moved out by the time I was in high school.

When my younger sister was 16, the eye doctor molested her. She came home and told me. We went together and told my parents. They did nothing.

I believe my parents not protecting me and not standing up for me affected me more than the actual molestation. I felt I experienced a double betrayal. In response to their lack of care and support, I believed I was worthless. I was not valuable.

I struggled with the lie that the molestation was my fault. Since I was dressed in a gypsy costume, maybe I was seductive and therefore I deserved it. I doubted myself.

Another issue I struggle with is overreacting with anger. When I feel misunderstood or not protected, I can overreact. When I was in grade school, I was accused of cheating on a test and sent to the principal's office. It wasn't true, and I became hysterical.

Another time, when my husband and I were in a hotel, he left the door unlocked. I had just gotten out of the shower and was putting lotion on, buck naked, and a man walked in our room. I screamed and he darted out the door. I was so angry at my husband for forgetting to lock the door. It truly was not intentional on his part, and it is normal to be angry about leaving the door unlocked. However, because of not being protected as a little girl from the molestation, I projected onto my husband and assumed that he wasn't protecting me either, so my anger was more complicated than just a reaction to an unlocked door. I know deep down that my husband would not do something intentionally to cause me harm.

I also struggle with control, especially with men. When I was working, I always had to be better than any man. I had to "one up" any man and needed to be on top of the success ladder.

I had the most wonderful experience with God as He started healing me in July of 1995 when I started reading and meditating on the book: *Names of God* by Kay Arthur. "El Roi" is "One Who sees." God saw what happened to me. He knew the truth. He knew it wasn't my fault. He cared about me.

Another spiritual practice that was healing to me is "Jesus Weeping over my Abuse." (It might be best if you do this one with your therapist). This is where I imagined being 10 again, in the garage, being molested. Jesus was there, too. He was weeping in the corner because of what was happening to me. He knows. He cares. I am valuable.

Now when I overreact, I do a spiritual exercise where I un-pack the anger with God.

- I sit in a quiet place and ask God for His wisdom (James 1:5).

- I go over the event and ask, "Is there any justification?" For example, with the hotel incident, I can feel angry about some strange man walking in my room, especially when I am naked. I can be upset with my husband for forgetting to lock the door. But accusing my husband of not protecting me, of me not being valuable to him, or of him not caring for me is an overreaction because of the molestation.

- I can go deeper and uncover the lie: I am not worthy.

- Then I can surrender this lie to God and replace it with truth: "My husband does love me; it was an accident. God loves and values me. I am worthy."

A relative passed away and we had a family funeral. Another family member, who molested some of the girls in our family, wanted to come to the funeral. This created a big feud over whether he should be allowed to come or not. The girls he molested would be there and this would be extremely uncomfortable for them. My husband confronted him one day and said he would not be allowed to come to the funeral. What my husband did really touched my heart. I experienced redemption from seeing a man protect me and other women.

Shame

There is a difference between toxic shame and shame that leads to conviction. Healthy conviction comes from the Holy Spirit. Toxic shame comes from the enemy or from our own critical voice. Shame affects our self-worth. Jesus was honest about people's sin however, He never attacked their self-worth. He always treated them as valuable even when they sinned. He values us, too. He doesn't shame you or blame you for the abuse. He wants you to be honest about your current behavior and take responsibility. Below is a brief description and some examples of toxic shame and healthy conviction.

Toxic Shame

Not sure what I did wrong

Leads to feelings of low self-worth

Draws me away from God, feel unloved

Self-deprecation, lack of self-love

Healthy Conviction

Clearly know I what I did wrong

Leads to repentance, to change

Leads to a feeling of being loved by God

Healthy self-acceptance and self-worth

Examples of Toxic Shame:

I am not good enough.

I am not valuable.

I am a loser.

I am not significant.

Nobody likes me.

I have no talents.

I am a lousy parent, friend, spouse, etc.

I deserve crap.

It's all my fault. I deserved the abuse.

Examples of Healthy Conviction:

I yelled at _____, I need to apologize.

I sinned, I need to ask forgiveness.

I lied about _____. I need to be honest.

I have been critical of _____ behind their back, and in my head, I need to stop this thought and take it captive to Christ.

I have been blaming _____, for _____. I need to look at and own my part.

I have been beating myself up, I need to embrace that I am His beloved and there is no more condemnation in Christ.

Truth: I was hurt. It was assault.

I am not to blame for what happened to me. I was a victim of the abuse.

It wasn't sexual; it was about power and control.

It was not my fault.

It did happen to me. I don't need to hide.

I am worthy, as God's daughter, of His love, to be loved and to love.

With God's help, I can let go of the past and experience freedom.

With God's help, I can take responsibility for my behavior that was a result of abuse.

Identifying Your Shame

Write down what is going on in your head. Don't judge it, edit it or criticize it. _____

_____

_____

_____

Review what you have written. Are these "thoughts/voices" in your head healthy? Or toxic?

_____

_____

_____

If it's healthy, ask God for wisdom as to what your next step is. _____

_____

_____

_____

If it's unhealthy, what truth do you need to replace it with? _____

_____

_____

On the next page is an Imaginative Prayer exercise with the bleeding woman. I love how Jesus does not judge her for her condition, because back then women were considered unclean during their periods and therefore shunned. I am not sure how old she was, only that she was hemorrhaging for 12 years. She could have been older than Jesus, who was in His early thirties. He didn't treat her as an outcast but showed compassion and offered healing. The best part for me is when He lovingly calls her *Daughter*.

Healed by Touching Christ's Garment by Alexandre Bida

As Jesus was on His way, the crowds almost crushed Him. And a woman was there who had been subject to bleeding for twelve years, but no one could help her. She came up behind Him and touched the edge of His cloak and immediately her bleeding stopped.

"Who touched me?" Jesus asked. When they all denied it, Peter said, "Master, the people are crowding and pressing against you." But Jesus said, "Someone touched me, I know that power has gone out from me."

Then the woman, seeing that she could not go unnoticed, came trembling and fell at His feet. In the presence of all the people, she told why she had touched Him and how she had been instantly healed.

Then He said to her, "Daughter, your faith has healed you. Go in peace."

Luke 8:40-48

Imaginative Prayer Exercise

Imagine you are in this scene as a part of the crowd. What do you see? Hear? Smell? What are you feeling as you see Jesus among the crowd? Now Jesus wants to know who touched Him. And this woman comes and falls at His feet. What is going on inside you?

_____

_____

_____

Do you feel compassion towards her? Or some judgment for sneaking up on Jesus like that? Or some criticism since she is a "bleeding" woman? Or maybe a little of both?

_____

_____

_____

Now imagine you are the bleeding woman. What is your bleeding? What is your shame?

_____

_____

_____

Do you desire to touch Him? If you desire to be touched by Jesus, allow His healing power to enter you and heal you.

Write down any trembling you are feeling. What is keeping you from "touching" His cloak? Or admitting you need His healing? _____

_____

_____

Maybe you have been healed but fear is keeping you from sharing this in the crowd. What is holding you back? _____

_____

_____

How do you feel towards Jesus when He compassionately calls you "Daughter?" _____

_____

_____

How does that make you feel about yourself? _____

_____

_____

Go in peace. What peace is He inviting you into? _____

Pamela's Story

I grew up on a farm in Kentucky. I was #12 out of 13 children. On Sundays, the older siblings would take my mom to church and leave me home with my father and baby sister because our church had no nursery. As I grew older I noticed I hated Sunday mornings. I hated stairs and the basement in the house I grew up in. I did not like to be surprised. I choked more often than normal on simple food and drinks. I had chest pains that the doctors could find no reason for and I cringed when my father hugged me. As a child, I had no recollection of Sunday mornings and didn't know why I felt these things. One of the things I did remember was my father telling me I was just another mouth to feed.

My dad started abusing me when I was two. He would grab me from behind and take me to the basement. He did to me what no father should do. After therapy many years later, I could remember his penis in my mouth. I would choke and I pass out. He would hit me on my back; I would spit up semen and then regain consciousness. This was my Sunday morning until I was four. The abuse stopped when the rest of my family stopped going to church.

When I got married, I hated sex. I always felt dirty. Depression set in and I felt so unworthy and so empty. We had a daughter. Every day I would drop her off at school and then go to the mall. I filled this hole in me with things. Instead of drugs or alcohol, shopping became my addiction.

I started having suicidal thoughts. As I was driving one day, I decided to end my life. I had a plan to run my car off the cliff at a point where the road curved and there was no guard rail. As I approached the curve, I unbuckled my seat belt and rolled the windows down. Just before the curve, a voice said to me "Don't do it . . . your daughter needs you." I didn't care, all I wanted was to die. I was caught off guard by the voice and before I knew it, I missed the curve.

I struggled with low self-esteem, unworthiness, anger, and trusting others. A few months later God revealed the source of my feelings and depression. A friend invited me to go to her church. I resisted but God persisted and I went. A lady there gave me the name of a Christian psychologist and he helped me tremendously. Through therapy and healing prayer, I was able to re-call the abuse from my childhood. I suddenly understood why I hated stairs, hated sex, hated hugs from my father and choked on food and drinks more often than normal. Over time, God healed me and turned my life right-side up.

Some of the ways I experienced God's healing power was by writing a letter to my Dad, replacing lies with truth, and healing prayer. I wrote a letter to my Dad even though he was deceased and told him how he had hurt me. I just wrote and wrote and let all those feelings come out. Then I was able to write that I forgave him and that I loved him. I was able to forgive him for all he had done to me. I was set free of anger, bitterness and resentment.

I learned to replace the lies of unworthiness and self-hatred with biblical truths such as:

Lie: *I am unworthy*

Truth: *I am worthy by the blood of Jesus*

Lie: *I am just another mouth to feed*

Truth: *I am a child of God precious in His sight*

What Satan meant for evil, God turned into something good.

The *good* is that I have used my pain to help other women and men. I do public speaking and offer healing prayer. I became involved in healing prayer because I wanted to help other women become free of their abuse issues. Forgiveness is the KEY to deep healing.

I am so grateful for God's healing power in my life.

Meditation

Many scriptures tell us how much God loves us. I encourage you to meditate on a scripture. By spending the time in silence, focusing on the truth, then slowly it will sink into our hearts.

When you are feeling shame, try meditating on a truth or scripture. In order to gain the most from scripture meditation it is important to let God help you identify your core lie or lies. We all have at least one and it has no doubt affected our lives for a long time. Remember, when we slowly meditate on God's word, *it lingers*.

Core Lies We Believe:

I am not worth being protected.

I am not enough.

I am unlovable.

I have no value.

I am just a/an_____.

How to Meditate:

- Find a comfortable, silent, and safe place.
- Relax your body. Breathe deeply in and out.
- Ask God to identify your core lie.
- Focus on your truth or scripture (e.g. I am God's Beloved or I am worthy).
- When thoughts enter in, *and they will*, put them in an imaginary cupboard.
- Focus again on your truth.
- Give this at least 10 min. Practice this daily if possible.

On the next few pages are a list of scriptures put together by Freedom in Christ Ministries. Here are some of my favorite scriptures to meditate on:

I am a child (daughter) of God. John 1:12
I am no longer condemned since Christ is in me. Romans 8:1
I am fearfully and wonderfully made. Psalm 139:13-14
I am His beloved daughter with whom He is well pleased. Mark 1:13
I am so loved by God that nothing can separate His love from me. Romans 8:38-39
I am valued. Matthew 6:26

What are some of your favorite scriptures?

In Christ . . .

I AM SIGNIFICANT:

Matthew 5:13	I am the salt of the earth.
Matthew 5:14	I am the light of the earth.
John 1:12	I am God's child (1 John 3:1-3).
John 15:1, 5	I am a branch of the true vine, a channel of His life.
John 15:16	I have been chosen and appointed to bear fruit.
Acts 1:8	I am a personal witness of Christ's.
1 Cor. 3:16	I am God's temple.
1 Cor. 12:27	I am a member of Christ's body
2 Cor. 5:17, 18	I am a minister of reconciliation for God.
2 Cor. 6:1	I am God's co-worker (1 Cor. 3:9).
Eph. 1:1	I am a saint.
Eph. 2:6	I have been raised up and am seated with Christ.
Eph. 2:10	I am God's workmanship.
Phil. 3:20	I am a citizen of heaven (Eph. 2:6).

I AM ACCEPTED:

John 15:15	I am Christ's friend.
Romans 5:1	I have been justified.
1 Cor. 6:17	I am joined to the Lord and am one spirit with Him.
1 Cor. 6:20	I have been bought with a price. I belong to God.
1 Cor. 12:27	I am a member of Christ's body.
2 Cor. 5:21	I have been made righteous.
Eph. 1:5	I have been adopted as God's child.
Eph. 2:18	I have direct access to God through the Holy Spirit.
Eph. 2:19	I am of God's household.
Eph. 2:19	I am a fellow citizen with the rest of the saints.
Eph. 3:12	I may approach God with boldness and confidence.
Col. 1:14	I have been redeemed and forgiven of all my sins.
Col. 2:10	I am complete in Christ.

I AM SECURE

John 1:12	I am a child of God (Gal. 3:26-28).
Rom. 8:28	I am assured that all things work together for good.
Rom. 8:35	I cannot be separated from the love of God.
Rom. 8:1	I am free forever from condemnation.
Rom. 8:33	I am free from any condemning charges against me.
2 Cor. 1:21	I have been established, anointed and sealed by God.
Eph. 1:13, 14	I have been given the Holy Spirit as a pledge, guaranteeing my inheritance to come.
Col. 1:13	I have been delivered from the domain of darkness and transferred to the kingdom of Christ.
Col. 3:3	I am hidden with Christ in God.
Phil. 1:6	I am confident that the good work that God has begun in me will be perfected.
Phil. 4:13	I can do all things through Him who strengthens me.
2 Tim. 1:7	I have not been given a spirit of fear but of power, love and a sound mind.
Heb. 4:16	I can find grace and mercy in time of need.
1 John 5:18	I am born of God and the evil one cannot touch me.

The Model of Jesus

Jesus did not shame people. He called them out on sins and idols but He did not attack their self-worth.

Jesus didn't yell at or criticize the bleeding woman for touching his cloak. Instead He healed her, called her *daughter*, and said, "Go in peace." (Luke 8:48).

He told the woman in adultery to sin no more. He did not shame her by telling her she was a whore (John 8:1-8).

He did not shame the woman who washed His feet with her hair. He appreciated what she did for Him. She was so filled with gratitude. He was not concerned with what the Pharisee thought since what she did was so inappropriate in those days (Luke 7:36-48).

He did not shame the woman at the well. He offered her living water. He did call out her five husbands and yet he did not tell her she was worthless (John 4).

Jesus didn't tell Zacchaeus that he was disgusting. In those days people despised tax collectors. Instead He invited Zacchaeus to have dinner with him (Luke 19).

He did not shame Peter when He predicted His death and Peter said the crucifixion would never happen to Him. He confronted Satan instead (Luke 21-23).

He told Peter he would deny Him but didn't say that he was bad, no good, a lousy friend, stupid, worthless, or not good enough. He offered him reconciliation in love (John 21).

He did not shame Judas for betraying him. He allowed him to make a choice.

He didn't tell Thomas that he was stupid for doubting. He offered him to put his hand in His side so he would believe (John 20:24-29).

He didn't tell the thief on the cross that he was a loser. Jesus offered him paradise. (Luke 23:39-43).

He didn't call the Rich Young Ruler arrogant. He asked him to follow him and spoke truth to him about his idol of riches. Jesus loved him (Mark 10:21, Matthew 19:16-23).

Jesus took on our shame on the cross. (When I was in Israel, the tour guide told me that people were stripped naked in those days when they were crucified). Jesus experienced shame and yet He did not let that stop Him. Three days later, He arose. His wounds were present, yet healed, and He moved on.

Jesus took thoughts captive. He knew who He was. His identity was firm. He was grounded in God. He and the Father were tight; they were one. Jesus didn't let others shake His identity. He did not allow shame or self-deprecation to rule His life. He desired what God desired, all the way to the end.

He offers you a new life and new way of being. He offers you significance, acceptance, worthiness and above all eternal love.

Jesus doesn't shame me.

He doesn't shame you.

Shame keeps us in bondage to feelings of unworthiness. Identifying your shame and sharing it with someone breaks the "secret", the bondage, so you can embrace the truth that you are worthy. You are a child of God, deeply valued and loved by Him.

Christ took on our shame when He died for our sins. It's done. We no longer have to live a life of not being good enough. Once the lie has been revealed, we can begin the process of replacing lies with truth. Meditation is a tool to allow the truth in our heads to slowly permeate throughout our body, our soul and into our hearts. If we will take the time alone with God, He will transform our shame into worthiness, into love, into beauty. As the outer layers of my shame are peeled away, there is the best place, my heart. I am created to be an encourager and listener, offering gifts of compassion, love and generosity. I am so worth it.

And so are you!

Chapter Five
Anger

Anger is a human emotion we all feel at times. It warns us when we are in danger. It alerts us when we are triggered about something. God expressed anger at times throughout the Old Testament. Jesus also expressed anger when He confronted the Pharisees' arrogance, the merchants in the temple and when His disciples fell asleep while with Him in the Garden of Gethsemane.

Sadly, many women I know, including myself, learned growing up that anger is bad. In my generation, a woman is generally considered "crazy" or a "bitch" when she expresses any anger. I learned growing up from both my family of origin and my culture that being angry was not ok. In order to survive, I learned how to stuff it or run away from it. I saw anger as rejection.

My Dad was a rage-aholic. He often took it out on my mother and us daughters. Being the youngest, I learned how to run and hide. I also ran away from Mr. Berger when he approached me. This behavior served me well as a child but not as an adult. I started noticing bursts of anger explode from my mouth at times. I would emotionally withdraw from someone who was angry with me. I avoided conflict and saw it as rejection. I later realized I was overreacting because of my childhood wounds. I learned that deep pain lies beneath that overreaction in anger. I will share some of my insights and learnings with you in this chapter.

Part of my healing process was forgiving my father for the way he expressed his anger towards me. I had to grieve over never hearing that I was his precious beloved daughter…something that I so desperately needed. Hearing my dad's story helped me in my forgiveness process. As I listened to his story, I could see how he too was wounded by life and where all his rage came from. He was not allowed to express his anger growing up. Although I do not condone his behavior, I did feel compassion for him. I would like to share his story with you.

My Dad's Story

Life was tough growing up for my father. His parents were teenagers when they immigrated to the United States from Russia during the Bolshevik Revolution in the early 1900s. They left their homeland and came to America in hope of a better life. They settled in Palo Cedro, California and became farmers. My grandfather worked hard raising cattle, horses and chickens. He owned several acres of wheat which needed to be cared for on a daily basis. There were no tractors in those days, just horses and a plow. My grandmother worked hard in the home with the daily chores and raising the children. She gave birth to ten children in her lifetime. Only five survived into adulthood.

My dad was the second oldest son. His brother Nick was the firstborn and they were close. After milking the cows (at 4:30 in the morning) they would eat their mom's delicious homemade bread and then go play the fields. In the summer, swimming in the creek was so much fun after finishing the chores. My dad told me how they gathered sticks to play cowboys and Indians. He looked up to Nick, his older brother.

Then one day, when my dad was eight years old, he, Nick, and some other boys were playing in an open field. They would throw a ball against a wall made of brick and rocks, and try to catch it as it bounced back. My dad's cousin was driving a Ford truck down the hill when suddenly the brakes failed and he lost control. The truck plowed into the field where the children were playing, pinning Nick against the wall. He let out a bloodcurdling scream. My dad said he stood there, helpless, and watched his brother slowly die.

My dad's parents did not show emotion. Grief and anger were not allowed. They had to be tough. They had to survive. Life on the farm went on.

Many illnesses were present in those days, some that we don't see today, thanks to modern medicine. Diphtheria entered their home. My dad's younger brother, Alex, who was two, was not strong enough to fight off the disease. He died one day in his mother's arm.

Life went on as usual. There was work to be done. My dad told me how one of his jobs was tending to the chickens. Part of his job was keeping the rooster away from the chickens so they could lay unfertilized eggs. One day my grandfather rushed into the hen house where my dad was, saying they couldn't find his three-year-old sister Olga. They all searched frantically around the farm. My dad went into the barn where the cows were. They had a trough filled with milk. As he looked into the trough, there was his little sister, face down. Beside her was a kitten. The kitten went after the milk and Olga went in after the kitten. Both drowned that day.

My dad was very close to another brother, Andy. He told me how they would trap skunks together. When they trapped a skunk, they would throw stones on it until it sprayed the entire stink out. On one occasion, thinking the skunk was all done spraying, my dad slowly approached the skunk. Then suddenly *blast*! It got him and he stunk badly. Andy and my dad laughed all the way home until their mother got a whiff. She put Dad in a bath of tomatoes. He could hear Andy chuckling from the other room. Andy continued to tease him about it for days. Dad really liked Andy.

World War II came upon them. Dad remembered the day Pearl Harbor was bombed. He and Andy couldn't wait to enlist. It was an honor in those days to serve our country, especially during war. Every capable man enlisted after the Japanese bombed Pearl Harbor. Dad remembered the day they said good bye to one another as each left home to serve in the military.

My dad became a pilot and flew PBY airplanes. Andy was stationed in London. Then one day, the call came that a bomb had struck Andy's platoon. He died that day along with his fellow soldiers. Times were tough in those days. They could not afford to bring his body home for burial, so Andy was buried in a military cemetery outside of London. I can't imagine how my grandmother felt when she lost another child and couldn't even bury him with the rest of the family.

When the war ended my dad settled in to find a career. He was in his mid-twenties when he got another of the far too frequent, dreadful phone calls. His father had been hit and killed by a bus while crossing the street.

My grandmother remained a widow until she died at 52 of high blood pressure. I believe she actually died of a broken heart.

Dad told me on several occasions about an aunt who was very strict. She would pull his hair and call him "*Ah- hol*" (not the right spelling but pronounced like "a—hole") which in Russian means "you will never amount to anything." That stuck with my dad all those years. He was so angry at her and was going to prove her wrong. I think what this aunt said to him, combined with all the death in his family that he was not allowed to grieve, was the reason my Dad became a rage-aholic. I am not excusing his behavior. I am just saying I get it. And on his deathbed, I told my dad that he was not an "*ah-hol*" and that I loved him.

Finally, I heard him say, "I love you, too, honey."

I can honestly say I have forgiven my dad. I am able to reflect on the good stories of his childhood that he shared with me. I am able to express gratitude for all the good things he did during my childhood. He was a moral man, a good provider for our family, and often went out of his way to help me. I will look forward to seeing him in heaven.

Women who have been emotionally, physically or sexually abused feel a deep sense of anger. You have a right to feel anger towards someone who has abused you. What they did was terribly wrong. It is not wrong or bad for you to be angry or to feel angry. It is healthy to explore, manage and express anger in an appropriate way. Often what happens is that we stuff, explode or displace our anger. I have done this at times. I was not allowed to express any negative feelings as a child, especially anger. I learned how to handle anger from my father. I am not blaming him as I take full responsibility for my actions as an adult. What I am saying is that I am aware of why I can stuff anger and how it can erupt like a volcano occasionally. Just as lava can destroy a city, unhealthy anger can lead to disruption and ruin our relationships. I hear from many other women on how difficult handling anger can be. At least I know I am not alone.

At times, we may be overreacting because of a repressed wound. Displaced anger is being angry at someone who is not the real problem. Sometimes, a woman (or man) yells at a child but is really mad at her spouse. Or she explodes at the spouse about not picking up his socks but is really mad about how he spends too much money. Inappropriate anger is an overreaction to a person or situation. I can be overly angry at people, especially men who are controlling, since my father was controlling.

Initially when we experience anger, there often is another feeling which lies beneath such as hurt, shame, fear or frustration. Sometimes we are not aware of the hurt we carry. We have a hard time admitting we are afraid or frustrated so we stay angry. Sometimes we fool ourselves into thinking we are in control by staying angry. Yet we are only hurting ourselves.

Therefore, we need to learn how to be angry. The first step is to admit our anger and recognize it our bodies. Then we can explore what truly lies beneath the anger. From that place, we can decide what to do with it.

Scripture tells us to "be angry and do not sin in our anger" (Eph. 4:26). It is ok to be angry. It is ok to be angry at God. He is a big God. He can take it. Some people are very uncomfortable with being angry at God and even feel it's sinful. Yet, David was angry at God in the Psalms. And scripture tells us that he was a man after God's heart. David was open and honest with God. He loved God deeply and had tremendous faith. If David can lament to God, then so can I. And so can you.

The Body

Our bodies are a wealth of information. Our body signals us when something is right and when something is wrong. Although I do not have training in body work, I do know several trauma therapists and wellness practitioners who do.

Mary Byrne Hoffman is a spiritual director and wellness practitioner. [11] According to her studies, research has shown that trauma is stored in the limbic brain located at the lower back of the head. The limbic brain stores and processes both emotions and memories. When a person is abused, that experience becomes lodged in the limbic brain which governs major physiological functions: the heart, the immune, digestive, reproduction and hormonal systems. The result is that stored trauma not only has emotional, psychological and spiritual consequences, it also affects our physical well-being since the limbic brain doesn't access language or rational thinking. Talk therapy has a limited long-range success with trauma. Both the spiritual and creative practices, with incorporating the body, will help bring about a more complete, long range healing.

Women have shared in group how they can feel emotions trapped in their body. One felt rapid heart beating when being with God in silence and solitude. She was raped at gun point in a place that was silent. I personally found silence and solitude very healing although I do know it can be scary for some. Another woman shared how she cringes when people touch her. She knew that trauma was trapped in her body and desired to be healed. Another shared she could not do any practices that imagine sitting on God's lap as that is how she was molested by her perpetrator. Pamela shared with us how she hated sex and had to work through that as she did want to have an intimate relationship with her husband. Several women have told me how they needed to explore the truth that our bodies were made for pleasure. Guilt and shame dominated their reactions since the sexual assault brought pleasure even though this was abusive. Several women have received help through body trauma therapy and EMDR (Eye Movement Desensitization and Reprocessing) with a licensed therapist.

I encourage you to listen to your body. It is trying to tell you something. There is healing how there for those of you who store trauma in your body. You are not crazy. And you are definitely not alone.

On the next page is an Imaginative Prayer exercise. Ask God to reveal to you what feelings, particularly anger, reside in your body. Then we will explore anger and unpack the feelings that lie beneath along with our deeper needs.

Imaginative Prayer Exercise

> In the temple courts, He (Jesus) found men selling cattle, sheep and doves and others selling at tables exchanging money. So He made a whip out of cords, and drove all from the temple area, both sheep and cattle; He scattered the coins of the money changers and overturned tables. To those who sold doves He said, "Get out of here! How dare you turn my Father's house into a market!"
>
> John 2: 14-16 (NIV)

- Sit with God in silence. Imagine you are in the temple with Jesus. What do you see?
- As an observer, how are you feeling about what is going on?
- Allow yourself to feel angry. What are you really angry about in your life?
- Close your eyes and scan through your body slowly. What part feels angry?
- Identify how the anger feels in your body:

chest tightens   jaw clenches   face scrunches   shallow breathing   shoulders tense

stomach tightens   head hurts   back tenses   heart pounds   palms sweat   other symptoms

- Make peace with your body as it is telling you what is really going on inside.
- Accept the part of you that is angry and tell yourself that you are ok, loved and accepted.

When I feel anger in my body, I will take a walk and pound the pavement with my feet. Or I will journal all my raw, true authentic feelings. I have had women "swear at the chair" during a session which is imagining the person who hurt you is sitting there and you can tell them exactly how you feel. Another idea is to have a pillow fight. Go to the gym and use a punching bag. Try to find a healthy and safe way to release the anger in your body. Or as I mentioned earlier, seek help through a trauma therapist.

Unpacking Anger

I remember long ago when I overreacted to my boss's anger and was not aware of why at the time. He was angry over a mistake I made and I apologized. Yet I was triggered, overreacted and turned in my two-week resignation. I truly regretted that decision and beat myself up that I overreacted. As I reflect on that now, his anger triggered that faulty belief in me that anger is bad, I am not valuable, and therefore need to run away to protect myself. That is what I did as a little girl. Running away was helpful as a child but destructive as an adult.

Amber: *I struggle with overreacting with anger when I feel misunderstood or not protected. When I was in grade school, I was accused of cheating on a test and sent to the principal's office. It wasn't true and I became hysterical. Then another time I blew up like a volcano at my husband when he accidentally left our hotel room unlocked. A strange man walked in while I was standing there buck-naked putting lotion on after my shower.*

Clara: *I had so much resentment, anger, bitterness and judgment towards my stepfather. I developed a bitter root judgment towards my mother. I notice I can be overly angry with people.*

Pamela: *I was so depressed and angry at myself. I felt so unworthy that I wanted to end my life.*

Darla: *I saw so much anger in our church from women who had been abused. They became control freaks.*

Maddison: *I was so angry that my mom and the therapist did not believe me.*

Most people would be upset to be falsely accused of something. Most of us feel angry over injustice. What you want to explore is when you become hysterical like Amber or overreact like I did with my boss. This kind of anger can show up as being displaced or out of proportion. There was some validity to our anger, however, it was more than what the experience called for.

Anger is a secondary emotion. Usually there are other feelings that lie beneath anger. Three common emotions that lie beneath are hurt, fear and frustration.

When hurt is the primary emotion, one needs to enter forgiveness to heal. When fear is the primary emotion, one needs to be empowered, to have courage. When frustration is the primary emotion, one needs to problem solve.

The Uncaged Project by Sallie Culbreth[12]

Was I feeling hurt? About what? _____

Am I feeling shame? _____

Was I feeling fear? About what? _____

Am I feeling frustrated? Why? _____

We will discuss forgiveness in Chapter Twelve and Fear in Chapter Six. For now, I encourage you to explore your deep core needs and desires. This is not about condemnation or feeling bad about yourself. (Romans 1:8 *Now there is no more condemnation in Christ*). This is about being aware of what is going on inside. Often, we are angry because a deep need isn't being met.

Common deep needs are:

I need to be loved.	I want to be understood.	I need to accomplish.
I want to feel valued.	I want to be in control.	I want appreciation.
I want to be significant.	I want to feel hopeful.	I need to have a purpose.
I want to be effective.	I want to feel worthy.	I want attention.
I want to belong.	I need security.	I need to feel safe.
I want respect.	I need to be heard.	I need recognition.

Ask God to reveal to you what it is you need and what you are seeking. Sometimes we are angry at people or a circumstance because our deep need isn't being met. I use to get angry at certain people for not listening to me. My deeper need was to be heard. I realized that listening is a gift which not many people have. Now I have more realistic expectations and seek out a good listener when I have something deeper to share. And God is the one who always listens. Remember it is ok to have your deep needs. We often need to change our expectations, which I will discuss more in Chapter Ten.

Sometimes we have hidden anger towards ourselves. This type of anger is different from depression, which needs to be treated in counseling. Anger at myself can be a form of "beating myself up" or blaming myself for the situation that has caused anger. Children of abuse tend to blame themselves for what happened to them. Adult women who have experienced rape, date rape, and molestation also can blame themselves. In the case of abuse, the person was a victim and subject to someone else's need for power and control. Sexual abuse is not about sex. It's about power and control. Often, abused victims carry this victim mentality into adult life and blame themselves or others for every wrong thing that happens. This victim mentality needs to be broken. We don't have to stay victim to our past. We can take responsibility for our actions as adults and begin a recovery process. We can learn how to acknowledge and own our part, which leads to maturity and freedom.

I was once angry at a person whom I let get too close to me. I didn't see the red flags initially and then I chose to ignore them when I did. I really wanted this relationship to work. This person became too possessive. When I realized it wasn't safe, I pulled away, causing much pain for the other person. My psychologist told me that because of my abuse, I tended to stay in unhealthy relationships too long. She said I needed to trust my intuition and the Holy Spirit inside me when I see those "red flags." I struggled with anger about that broken relationship for a long time. My spiritual director asked if I had anger towards myself and if I had forgiven myself for my choice. We did a prayer practice together where I asked God to show me why I chose this person and why I stayed in too long. I initially focused on the love I received and the fun we had which were valid needs of mine. I was able to forgive myself for "jumping in too quickly" and "staying in too long."

Take some time to journal about any insights into your anger and deeper needs.

_____

_____

_____

_____

_____

_____

_____

_____

_____

_____

One of my most healing practices has been Imaginative prayer with Jesus in the Garden (Mark 14:32-50). Below is a picture of the Garden of Gethsemane. When I was Israel, I was able to sit and reflect in the garden. I tried to imagine what it was like on that night Jesus prayed so diligently to God. The passage in Mark tells us He was overwhelmed to the point of death. The apostle Matthew tells us He was in such pain that he sweat blood.

Sitting in the pain and inviting God into that place is so hard and yet so necessary to heal. I remember crying about all the pain I had while God just held me in His arms. Depending on your pain, this may take some time. Although it causes me pain to see what Jesus went through, I also feel a sense of hope because He can identify with my suffering. He can identify with yours, too.

The Garden of Gethsemane
Photo taken by Ron Richardson, used with permission

Imaginative prayer on Jesus in the Garden

Read this passage slowly three times. You may want to gaze at the picture on of what the garden looks like today.

They went to a place called Gethsemane, and Jesus said to his disciples, "Sit here while I pray." He took Peter, James and John along with Him and He began to be deeply distressed and troubled. "My soul is overwhelmed with sorrow to the point of death," He said to them. "Stay here and keep watch."

Going a little farther, He fell to the ground and prayed that if possible the hour might pass from Him. "Abba, Father," He said, "Everything is possible for you. Take this cup from me. Yet not what I will but what you will."

Then He returned to His disciples and found them sleeping. "Simon," he said to Peter, "are you asleep? Could you not watch for one hour? Watch and pray so that you will not fall into temptation. The spirit is willing, but the body is weak."

Once more, He went away and prayed the same thing. When He came back He again found them sleeping because their eyes were heavy. They did not know what to say to Him. Returning the third time He said to them, "Are you still sleeping and resting? Enough! The hour has come. Look, the Son of Man is betrayed into the hands of sinners. Rise: Let us go. Here comes my betrayer!" Just as He was speaking, Judas, one of the Twelve, appeared. With him was a crowd armed with swords and clubs, sent from the chief priests, the teachers of the law, and the elders.

Now the betrayer had arranged a signal with them: "The one I kiss is the man; arrest Him and lead Him away under guard." Going at once to Jesus, Judas said, "Rabbi!" and kissed Him. Then one of those standing near drew his sword and struck the servant of the high priest, cutting off his ear.

"Am I leading a rebellion," said Jesus, "that you have come out with swords and clubs to capture me? Every day I was with you, teaching in the temple courts, and you did not arrest me. But the scriptures must be fulfilled."

Then everyone deserted Him and fled.

Mark 14:32-50

I am going to make some assumptions here that I believe.

I believe that Jesus, fully God and fully human, felt the same emotions we feel as humans.

As I look at the model of Jesus, this is what I see:

He felt stress, overwhelmed and sorrow to the point of death.

He may have felt anger towards God the Father for having to go to the cross. He felt some resistance and possible fear since He asked God to take the cup away from Him.

He felt betrayed. And with a deceptive kiss.

He felt disappointment and frustration that the apostles did not stay awake with Him and pray.

He felt some anger when he said "Enough!" to his disciples for falling asleep again.

He felt sadness that they had to arrest Him with weapons, that they didn't trust His character that was not rebellious.

He felt hurt and abandoned by how many deserted Him in His biggest hour of need.

- Sit here a minute and write down the feelings you have regarding a hard situation you are in. _____
  _____
  _____

- Now imagine you are in the garden. You are watching this scene. What do you see? Smell? Hear? What does the garden look like?
- Now you see Jesus, in agony, praying. How do you feel?
- Is there someone who has betrayed, hurt or abandoned you?
- Are you in a circumstance that you are angry about? Talk to Jesus about it, expressing how you honestly feel about the experience.

_____
_____
_____
_____
_____
_____
_____
_____

- Now He invites you to join Him in the pain. If you are comfortable, allow His loving arms to wrap around you. You may have some questions for Him or requests, just as He asked the Father to take the cup away:

  Why didn't you protect me? Why did this happen to me? Why didn't you do anything?

- Sit with Him and allow Him to enter into your pain.

Jesus Christ in Garden of Gethsemane – iStock photo.

When you are ready, pray:

Please take my cup: _____ away. Yet not my will but Thy will.

Anger at God

Some people have a hard time being angry at God. They feel it's wrong to feel that way or God would be upset with them. I believe it is ok to be angry at God. David lamented throughout the psalms. Scripture says that David was a man after God's heart. He was honest with God when he was happy and full of praise, and also when he was in despair and angry at God. Here are a few to look at.

> God, how long are you going to stand there, doing nothing? Save me from their brutalities, everything I have got is being thrown to the lions.
> Psalm 35:17-18 (MSG)
>
> Pay them back in evil! Get angry, God! Down with these people.
> Psalm 56:7 (MSG)
>
> On no account let them escape; in your anger, O God, bring down the nations.
> Psalm 56:7 (NIV)

Laments of David are also found in Psalms 55, 56, 57, 68, 77, 88, 102, 120, and 140.

Write your own psalm of lament to God. Tell Him how you really feel about what happened to you or what is happening now. Ask Him why He allowed this to happen to you. Why didn't He stop it? Ask God, where were you when this what happening to me? Hold nothing back!

_____

_____

_____

_____

_____

_____

_____

_____

_____

_____

_____

_____

Expressing Anger to Someone Else

I will admit, this is a hard one for me. Dealing with conflict makes me anxious because it taps into rejection and hurt feelings. Yet, holding a grudge can hurt even more. I have learned how to handle conflict with God's help and the help of others. After I have done all of the above (exploring, reflecting, etc.), here is what I do.

- I pray about it. Ask God for wisdom if I need to say something or not. For example, trying to reason with a narcissist or someone with mental illness often just makes it worse.

- I get advice from someone who is wise, and I trust their opinion.

- I check in with my motive. Confrontation is about reconciliation, not retaliation.

- Meet in person if possible. Or talk on the phone. I do not use email. So much body language is lost. So much can be misunderstood. It has been very upsetting for me when I have received long hurtful emails. No more email for me.

- I use the Hamburger sandwich method. It has been around for years, was developed by a therapist, and I am not sure who to give the credit to. The upper bun states a positive about the relationship: "I need to talk to you about something because I care about you and our relationship."
The meat is the issue with my feelings: "When you raise your voice, it triggers something in me and I feel hurt."
The bottom bun is the solution: "When you are angry with me, please use a calm voice. This will help me know you care about me and will make our relationship better which is what I want, too."

- Give the outcome to God. There is always a risk. Sometimes I have done all the above, prayed on my knees, and still the relationship ended. Yet, sometimes, speaking the truth in love can help the relationship become more intimate.

In summary, remember, God is infinite. If you look at the stars at night, the universe is infinite. There is so much we cannot see and do not know. And God created all that! So too His love for you is infinite. Read Romans 8:38-39 and meditate on it. Nothing can separate you from His love. Not even your lament.

Anger is a human emotion that alerts us that something is wrong. We may be justified in our anger as some of us have been wounded deeply by others. Some of us have witnessed people being abused by others. Our culture, even our church culture, tell us it is wrong or bad to be angry. As women, we are taught to be quiet and gentle. Secretly we learn to stuff our anger or inappropriately explode. Sadly, my father went to his grave without ever dealing with his anger. I felt so much compassion for him and yet such sadness because he could have been happier in life.

David was authentic with God. He was able to both praise and be angry in the Psalms he wrote. He was real with his feelings. God wants us to be authentic with Him. He is a big God and He can handle our anger. It does not push Him away like it pushes others away. He allowed both David's psalms of praise and his laments to be printed in His word. It is OK to be angry…not to sin in your anger.

Jesus was angry at times, as we read about the temple story and the Garden of Gethsemane. Some say that Jesus showed righteous anger as the money changers were desecrating the temple. I agree and I also point out the personal anger He felt in the Garden when his disciples fell asleep when He needed them the most.

If David can lament, so can I. And so can you.

If Jesus can be angry, so can I. And so can you.

Hopefully the tools you learned in this chapter will help you to explore how it feels in your body and what lies beneath your anger, including any deeper needs. You have a God who can heal those wounded places in your heart, filling you with that peace that surpasses understanding. I know it sounds like a pat answer but it is true…only God can fill those deeper needs of mine and of yours.

As I mentioned earlier, sometimes fear lies beneath anger. We will look at fear in the next chapter.

Chapter Six
Fear

Fear, particularly the fear of rejection or failure, has held me back at times from trusting God with my call. Sometimes it's hard being vulnerable and yet I know from experience that others are truly helped when I am. I can get hooked into what other people think I should be or should do. And I don't want to suffer the pain of failure either. Stepping out and taking a risk has been a challenge for me. I have had to face my fears.

The fear I am talking about is not the same as a healthy fear that warns us of danger. For example, if I suddenly come upon a rattlesnake, fear in my body will warn me I am in danger. A healthy fear arises when faced with a person who is abusive or toxic. This is warning us to remove ourselves or set up healthy boundaries. Scripture tells us to fear God, which means a healthy respect. I am talking about the harmful kind of fear that keeps us stuck and in bondage, preventing us from being and doing all we are called to be and do.

God tell us over and over not to be afraid, just as He did with many people throughout the scriptures. Often, we read these verses and may even memorize them. Yet keeping this advice in our heads doesn't really melt away the fear. Having a raw, authentic conversation with God as to what we truly fear is the start. If we ask Him, He will begin to transform our fears into courage, into peace, into trust. I am not saying that you will never fear again. I certainly do. Yet I notice I don't stay stuck like I used to do. He helps me take small steps, often one day at a time, toward my call. I find it freeing when I honestly admit my fears, reflect on the deeper issues, and then ask God for strength and courage. Even Jesus had to often tell His closest disciples not to be afraid. I am so grateful He didn't condemn them for being afraid and He doesn't condemn you or me either. Instead, He promises He will strengthen us when we turn to Him.

And that is just what I finally did. I created this workbook and started coming alongside other women who have been abused. My desire in this chapter is to share how God, over time, has transformed my fears into courage and into faith. First, I want to share Mariah's story with you. Her fear melted into courage as she realized she had a voice.

You have a voice, too.

Mariah's Story

I was born in Africa. When I was four, my parents migrated to Italy since my mom was Italian. This is where I grew up.

My twin sister and I were sheltered. We would play in the balcony and said "hi" to everyone who walked by. I remember the wonderful times we had at the beach. When my parents went out, they entrusted us to some friends, a couple who had a beautiful garden and a pond full of fish. We loved the joy the garden and fish gave us as little girls.

Yet, the man was a perpetrator. In their living room, they had little beds. When we would lie down to take a nap, he would lay down with us. He fondled us and then made us fondle him. This went on for a while. We witnessed each other's abuse.

One day, we both started crying to our parents that we don't want to go over there anymore. My parents did go over there and talk to them but they denied it. We never went over there again. I do remember being sad that I could no longer go into the garden and watch the fish.

Then it happened again with a different perpetrator. We were eleven. Paulo was a good friend of the family and our godparent. My dad traveled a lot. I couldn't prove it but I felt like there was something going on between my Paulo and my mother. One night they called and needed my mother to help them with their sick baby. She went over there and he came over to stay with us. We were in bed and he climbed in and lay in the middle between us. I laid still, frightened…pretending to be asleep. He turned over towards me and started to molest me. Then he wanted me to touch him. I resisted so he turned over and started to touch my sister. Anger erupted inside me and I jumped him. I told him he better leave my sister alone. He was surprised and he stopped.

In the morning, I told my mother exactly what happened. I told her that Paulo needs to stop coming over to our house or I was going to tell my dad. He denied everything and my mom believed him. I confronted her that she was having an affair with him and she denied it. This created some guilt in me as maybe I made a mistake. I struggled with this being my fault.

I was enraged. I stuffed my anger. In my helplessness, I opened the linen closet one day and shred everything with scissors. My mom didn't punish me. I just felt so betrayed.

When I was thirteen, I had a boyfriend, Antonio. One day, Paulo caught us fooling around. Being a virgin in Italy back then was a big deal and very important to the family. He told on me to my mother and I told her that Antonio and I were just making out and there was no intercourse and I was still a virgin. She didn't believe me. I became so angry that she chose to believe him over me. I felt betrayed all over again. My mom continued to be in denial.

Then I found out that Paulo was molesting his daughter. I lost it. I told my father everything…the abuse…my mom's affair…her denial…all of it. My father was stunned. He looked at my mom and she again was in denial. He looked at me and said it wasn't his place to deal with this. I sunk so low. I wasn't even protected by my own dad.

I did find the courage to send Paulo a four-page letter calling him every name in the book. I told him I was going to have him arrested if he ever came near me again. He never came over after that.

I had to deal with that anger all my life. Healing started in therapy when I was in my twenties. I had repressed the earlier incidents when were four-five years old. I expressed to my therapist about feeling guilty about finding pleasure in the molestation and she said that our bodies were made for pleasure but what both Paulo and our neighbor did to me was abusive.

Through time, with therapy and doing meditation and forgiveness exercises, I was able to release the anger towards both men who molested me. I also had to deal with the shame and guilt because the sexual stimulation felt good. My therapist helped me understand that our bodies are made for pleasure. The action taken against me was wrong and was not my fault. Overtime, I was able to release the guilt I felt and embrace my body.

It has taken longer to forgive my mother as I felt so betrayed by someone who was supposed to believe me, hear me, and protect me. I had this repetitive dream that I was trying to call my mother. She is with her lover. No one will help me and give me her phone number. I felt desperate as needed to talk to her. I am deeply hurt as she chose her lover over me. As I reflected on my dream, I realize that I felt the need to talk to her…to have her hear my voice…and yet feel devastated that she did not. On my mother's death bed, I was able to look at her and tell her I forgave her. I do not feel angry towards my mother now. Yet at times I do feel the sadness over what I did not receive from her.

A pivotal moment in my life happened when I was called for jury duty. The case was child molestation. I was able to be unbiased as a juror and listen to both sides presented. The evidence was beyond a reasonable doubt and we found him guilty. I felt a relief that justice was served for this girl. Even though I didn't get justice, I was happy I could be a part of her receiving justice.

Her name was also Mariah.

Recently, I traveled to Santa Cesarea in Italy. The legend of St. Cesarea happened long ago. She was a young girl who lived with her mother and stepfather. He was a perpetrator and was after her. An angel appeared and guided her to hide in the sea caves. Then the angel created a fog so that the stepfather could not find her. Since he could not see where he was going, he slipped, fell into the deep sea waters and drowned. A sulfur smell emerged because he was a "stinker." The angel then guided Cesarea out of the cave and she was safe. Today, many hot springs surround the area and Santa Cesarea is known to be a place of healing. As I soaked in the warm, sulfur water, I did not notice the "stink" from my past as much. I felt relaxed and at peace as I bathed in the healing water.

I refuse to call myself a victim. I stood up to both perpetrators in my life, even if no one heard me. God heard me. When I see others who are being abused, I will stand up for them. Something I have learned through my life experience is…

I have a voice.

I came alongside as a spiritual director with Mariah for about four years. She was not a Christian. I cared about her and wanted to see her have peace and freedom in her life.

I remember her telling me about her experience with a particular Christian organization. She was volunteering for a group that feeds the homeless. The leaders told her that God does not love her because she doesn't believe in Jesus as God in flesh. She expressed how upset she felt about this. I listened and felt troubled about this as well.

Then the subject changed, and she told me how the birds flocked to her balcony every morning and drank and ate from the feeders she put out. They would sing and make beautiful music. This brought her much joy. She felt this was God's gift to her.

The next day, during my prayer time, I remembered some sermons in the past that do preach about the "chosen ones" and that God only sees those who have accepted Jesus as Lord. I cried out to Him and said, "Really, God? Do you only see those who believe in Jesus? Aren't we all children of God? Doesn't your scripture say you loved the whole world and wish none would perish? What about all these people who have had near death experiences and come back to say that Jesus was there on their death bed…waiting for them? You are so infinite and so beyond my limited mind. Isn't there a lot we don't know?? How do you feel about Mariah? Then I said, "Ok, God, it is time for me to be quiet and just listen to you."

After some moments of quiet, birds appeared outside my window and started singing.

Reflection on Identifying Fear

Take a moment and reflect on some common fears. Go to God in silence. Ask Him to help you admit to what you are truly afraid of. Remember He is there for you.

Common Fears:

I am a sinner. God does not love me.
God does not have time for me.
God will ask me to do something I don't want to do.
I feel God and other people will judge me if He knows who I really am.
I am afraid of risk.
I am afraid of rejection.
I am afraid of failure.
I am afraid of what other people will say or what they will think of me.
I am afraid I am not good enough, not gifted enough.
I am afraid I will not have enough _____ (money, health, love, friends, work, etc.)
I am fearful of _____ (new situations, spiders, heights, needy people, being used, etc.)

Mark what you identify with.

Is there something you identify with that is not on this list? _____
_____
_____

What are you afraid of not having? _____
_____
_____

What are you truly fearful of losing? _____
_____
_____

Where do you feel fear in your body? _____
_____
_____

What in your life do you feel powerless over? _____
_____
_____

Fear drives many other emotions: anger, shame, worry, anxiety, negativity, control.

What are your deeper needs? (You can refer to Chapter 5 for the deeper needs.) For example, if someone is worrying about money most of the time, the deeper need may be for security. Or if someone needs to be in control of their children, it could be so they look good to others as a successful parent with the deeper need being significance. They may also try to control their children to keep them from experiencing pain. Or someone may need to be authoritative so they can have control, with a deeper need for respect. This may take some time. Sit in silence and ask God for wisdom as to what your deeper need is.

_____

_____

_____

_____

_____

_____

_____

_____

Where in your life do you need to take charge and be empowered? _____

_____

_____

_____

_____

With whom do you need to use your voice? _____

_____

_____

_____

I was 20 years old. I just moved out into my own apartment. I had my own checking account and a car. I felt so proud of myself for being independent.

Then one night all that changed.

It was dark. I pulled up into the parking lot where I lived. I heard this voice in my head to drive around the block but I didn't pay attention to it. Out of nowhere, a man came up…held a gun at my head…and told me to keep quiet. Overwhelming fear filled my body. I froze up. I did as I was told while praying he wouldn't take my life. He took me to a desolate park. There he raped me repeatedly while holding a gun to my head.

When it was over, he took me back to the parking lot where I lived and dropped me off. I was alive but filled with shock and despair. I called the police. My parents came over and tried to console me.

Then the blame game started. I kept thinking I shouldn't have been wearing that dress or I should have driven around the block or I shouldn't have done this or that. A friend of my parents said to my mother that maybe this happened to me because of some sexual sin. The things people say! I was so hurt by that. Even though I knew in my head I was a victim, I felt in my heart that somehow this was my fault.

The trauma left a huge scar in my being, one that has held me back and ruled my life…until now.

I am almost 50. Although I had therapy over the years, I realized that deeper healing was needed. I joined a covenant group called *Not Alone*. Although it was very difficult looking at my issues, I had an amazing experience with God and the group. It was so hard to face my pain and realize how much the rape affected my behavior. I couldn't see my own blind spots. This group lovingly helped me without judgment for which I am so grateful. I walked away with not being so stuck in fear as I was the past thirty years.

You see the rape completely changed the course of my life that I never could have imagined. I am sharing this because I want to be authentic, overcome fear and come alongside other women who are stuck in fear because of trauma. I see now how I wasn't authentic in my relationships as a wife, mother and friend because I wanted them to like me, not reject me. Now I am able to speak up and let others know I have needs, too. I also felt so much shame, especially body shame. I despised my own body and went on the roller coaster ride of gaining and losing weight for most of my life. I used to wear long sleeve shirts so I didn't expose my arms. Putting on a bathing suit was a nightmare. Just recently I wore a sleeveless dress. I also put on a bikini and jumped in our pool in my backyard. I felt so free. Now that I am at a healthy weight, I am able to take care of myself and enjoy my body.

What I learned is that I went on auto-pilot after the rape…just trying to survive. But I wasn't showing up with my desires, dreams, feelings and needs. I would tell myself that I couldn't do that or I am not good enough to do this. It's been a process and still is, but now I am so grateful to show up and be me. Recently, I accepted a volunteer position to lead a big parent organization at my son's school. Even though I still get nervous, I am able to speak at these meetings. At times I have to deal with conflict which I know is inevitable as the leader. I can handle this so much better than I did in the past.

Shame also kept me from talking about it. I tell women now to not keep it a secret. If something like this has happened, then go and tell someone. I have been on several T.V. shows to share my story. Recently I did a video on my Facebook. A few women have reached out to me. I am also writing a book about my story. I love coming alongside others who have had sexual trauma.

Earlier this year I felt the need to face one of my deepest fears. I went back to the parking lot where I was abducted. My heart was pounding and yet God showed up for me, giving me courage. We just sat together and grieved. God felt sorrow over what happened to me. I felt His comfort.

The rapist died in prison earlier this year. He was caught after raping 17 women. I was victim number four.

But I can now confidently say, "Number four, a victim no more."

The statue of Gabriel appearing to Mary at the Church
of Annunciation in Nazareth.

Imaginative Prayer: Mary, Mother of Jesus

As you read the following verses from the Message and NIV, slowly ponder it in your heart as if God is talking to you. You may use the pictures on the previous page for your reflection.

Read Luke 1:26-54, the story of Gabriel appearing to Mary.

> Gabriel greeted her (Mary): Good Morning!
>   You are beautiful with God's beauty
>   Beautiful inside and out!
>   God be with you!
>
>   Luke 1:28
>
> Do not be afraid. You will become pregnant and give birth to a son and call his name Jesus. He will be great, be called 'Son of the Highest.'
>   Luke 1:30-32
>
> (Mary's song) My soul glorifies the Lord and my spirit rejoices in God my Savior, for He has been mindful of the humble state of his servant. From now on all generations will call me blessed, for the Mighty One has done great things for me------Holy is His name.
>   Luke 1:46-49 (NIV)
>
> Nothing is impossible with God. And Mary said, 'Yes, I see it all now, I am the Lord's maid, ready to serve. Let it be with me, just as you say.'
>   Luke 1:37-38

Use your imagination to picture yourself there with Mary and Gabriel. Use your senses. What do you see? What do you hear? How do you feel about witnessing this event? How do you feel towards Mary? _____

_____

_____

Now imagine that Jesus is turning to you. He calls you beautiful. He created you, beautiful inside and out. He has shown favor on you. Allow yourself to feel His love and His favor.

What is 'birthing' in you? What is something new that Jesus is inviting you into? _____

_____

_____

_____

What are you afraid of? _____
_____
_____

Notice how Mary had tremendous courage to say "Yes" to God. She was 13 or 14, unwed and pregnant. This was not accepted in those days. Perhaps she was snubbed by others or her parents were disappointed she was pregnant out of wedlock. She had a miraculous experience with God that she stepped out in courage, regardless of what others would think or what might happen to her.

Where in your life do you need some courage? _____
_____
_____

Who are there people in your life that you are concerned what they think? _____
_____
_____
_____

Where is God with you in your place of fear? In your place of courage?
_____
_____
_____
_____

How does that make you feel about God? _____
_____
_____
_____

How do you feel about yourself right now? _____
_____
_____
_____

This was a powerful passage to me when I went through the Spiritual Exercises of St. Ignatius. I believed God was asking me to step up, take courage and tell other women my story and how He has done deep healing in my life. Following this, I started creating this workbook and gathering stories from women I have journeyed with. I couldn't have done this without Him. Like Mary, I treasure Jesus in my heart.

He can give you the courage you need.

Spiritual Practices and Prayers

Contemplative prayer with focused breathing

Close your eyes and imagine something that draws you to feel loved. I like to imagine the face of Jesus. Take 2-3 deep breathes. Breathe in God, breathe out worry. Breathe in Jesus, breathe out fear. Breathe in the Holy Spirit, breathe out control. Now breathe slowly and focus on your breathing and/or your image. Studies have shown that this has helped reduce anxiety since people can't focus on their struggles and their breathing at the same time. This is a good practice to do when you find yourself in an anxious or unsafe situation.

Breath prayers

Breath prayer is something you can say in one breath, either out loud or in silence. Below are some of my favorites. Try finding some of your own.

"O God, You are my strength." Psalm 18:1

"Perfect love casts out fear." 1 John 4:18

"I am your Beloved, on whom your favor rests." Mark 1:11

"I do believe; help me overcome my unbelief." Mark 9:24

"HELP!"

Chanting/Singing

Instead of saying a prayer out loud, try singing. Some people connect better with God when they sing or with music. Try singing a chorus of a favorite, soothing hymn.

> **"His love endures forever"**
>
> "Jesus Christ, Son of God, have mercy on me"
>
> "Yes, Jesus loves me. . ."

Reflecting Back

- Reflect on your life, the times you felt afraid. How was God there for you? How did you help you get through? You can use your story to help guide you.
- How did your faith strengthen you?
- How did God show He was trustworthy?
- What did God teach you through this? How have you grown?
- Remember how God was there for you in the past, in your current situation now.

The Model of Jesus

Jesus was not afraid to leave home at 30 to start his ministry. Jewish tradition was that the oldest son takes care of the family when the father dies. Jesus didn't do that. He followed His call and left home to go to Galilee. I believe that this is why Nazareth didn't welcome him back and why he wasn't close to his brothers and sisters (Matt.10:37, 11:46-50, 13:53-58).

Jesus was not afraid of Satan. He stood up to him in the desert with the power of the scripture (Matt. 4:1-11). He faced Satan again and again as he cast out demons (Matt. 4:1-11, Matt. 8:28-34).

Jesus was not afraid to break religious rules made by man. He healed the man with the shriveled hand on the Sabbath (Matt. 12:11-12).

He was not afraid to speak truth to the Pharisees. He often got in their face and told them they were vipers and hypocrites. He told them they were more concerned about the approval of man than pleasing God. They cared more about protecting their positions (Luke 11:37-54, Matt. 15:15-20, Matt. 23).

Jesus had courage to speak boldly about the kingdom of heaven. He declared that God's commandments outweighed the Pharisee's laws (Matt. 7:28).

Jesus was not afraid to challenge people to look deeper into God's commandments, to look into their hearts about murder and hate, adultery and lust, and the idol of money (Matt. 5:21, 27, 6:19).

Jesus was not afraid to hang out with sinners or go to their homes for a dinner party. He was not concerned with what others thought of him doing that (Mark 2:15-17).

Jesus was not afraid to speak truth to his friends. He rebuked Peter on Mt. Hermon (Matt. 17:7). He called them on their doubt and lack of faith. He also compassionately told them not to be afraid.

He was not afraid of rejection, of what others thought of Him. He went out of His way to speak to the Samaritan woman (John 4). He challenged the people to cast the first stone at the woman caught in adultery if they were without sin (John 8:1-11). He didn't care what the religious leaders thought of Him. He did the right thing anyway. He was not swayed from His purpose and His devotion to God.

He was not afraid of taking up his cross. He entered into the cross . . . even though He asked God to take the cup away (Matt. 26:42). He had tremendous courage and faith to do what He did.

He knew the disciples were afraid of when He first appeared to them after the resurrection. He encouraged them not to be afraid. He reconciled with Peter in love. He understood when Thomas doubted. He offered him to put his hands in His wounds (John 20-21).

And He didn't leave the disciples alone. He filled them with His Holy Spirit. From then on out, each of them was filled with amazing courage, even to the point of death. We see their courageous stories throughout the book of Acts. This very truth tells me the resurrection really happened and that Jesus truly is God in flesh. And He does not leave us alone either.

Peace--a word so commonly heard. "World Peace" in a speech. "Peace on Earth" in a Christmas card. "Peace Treaty" in a political speech. "Peace be with you" in a church service. We hear people talk of peace and yet sadly many of us do not experience internal peace. When we admit and then release our fears, we can truly have internal peace.

In summary, fear is something we all experience. Healthy fear warns us of danger and when we need to protect ourselves. Fear that leads to respect for God is a good thing. Explore how fear holds you back from being the real, true, beautiful you. Be aware of the fear that keeps you stuck from stepping out to follow your dreams. Admit your fears in a raw, authentic conversation with God. He can transform your fears into peace, into courage. You can have that *peace that surpasses all understanding* that the apostle Paul says in scripture.

You are here today with me on this journey because I released my fears and said yes to God. Trust God that He will give you what you need to get through whatever you are facing.

Chapter Seven
Control

Trauma can influence one to try to control their environment and their relationships in order to feel safe. The trauma that happened was out of our control. This contributes to a lack of trusting God to meet our needs, especially that core need of being loved and valued. Subconsciously God cannot be trusted and often neither can others, so we try to control everything and everyone around us. Women who are "control freaks" suffer with their relationships with God, others and themselves.

Most of us struggle with some degree of control. We want things to smoothly go our way. There is nothing wrong with this desire and yet life doesn't always turn out the way we wanted. It's how we respond to others, to God and to ourselves when our needs, hopes and dreams are not happening the way we wanted. Trying to control is one way to cope. However, this does not lead to peace, joy and freedom that comes with surrendering and letting go.

Surrendering control is necessary to receive transformation by God.

A colleague of mine is an alcoholic, sober for 30 years, and still active in AA. He said that one needs to surrender to God in order to truly change, to let go of all control. You can go to church, AA meetings, do good works and still not really surrender. I can see a genuine transformation in him. He is a beautiful combination of love, authenticity, and strength.

Darla came from a family of molestation that was passed down generationally. She is a pastor's wife who ministered to women who suffered from incest and became control freaks. As children, their home life was out of control. The pain these women experienced is beyond words. Let's read her story on the next page.

I was 10 years old. My best friend had a horse and one day we were in the corral together taking care of him. Suddenly we noticed there was this guy behind the bush. He was facing us, looking straight at us, while masturbating. We were afraid and knew we needed to get out of there. We felt we had to protect the horse so we took him with us. My mom was in shock when I showed up on my front door step with a horse.

My mom was horrified when I told her what happened. She called the police and filed a report. She was there for me in my hour of need. Although I only had this one limited exposure to a pervert, it bothered me for a long time. It creeped me out and then I thought all boys were creeps and they all had "cooties." This incident really did impact my opinion of men. I grew up with a control issue, saying to myself, "no man is going to do anything like this to me." I was driven to get my degree, not ever become a kept woman, and to take care of myself. I had to "one-up" men and I didn't ever want to be in an uncomfortable situation. I really didn't contribute my control issue to that event in the corral until much later.

The "much later" happened when my husband and I moved to pastor a church. We saw that our congregation was full of super-duper-control-freak women with passive husbands. I wanted to try and understand what that was about. I learned that about 9 out of 10 women had been sexually abused in my congregation. Most of this consisted of rape and abuse by fathers, brother, and uncles. There was stronghold bondage of incest in our community and in our church. Some women also had poor judgment. One woman took her children to the local river all the time and brought homeless people home with them. One of these homeless people molested her daughter and son. The son ended up acting out and the police were called. It turned out this boy had raped his own sister, and then ended up in the court system. Because of her past abuse, the woman's well-intentioned bad judgement ended up harming her own children.

As a pastor's wife, I felt overwhelmed with the sexual abuse issues in our church. I struggled with how to help them. Since this was a rural community, I called Focus on the Family for support. I received good counsel from them and they sent me materials to use. We started abuse support groups which were helpful for women to be able to share in a group. Some of the best advice I learned, as a pastor's wife and lay counselor is:

First, do not compare the degree of transgression. Don't say some sexual events are worse than others. The age of the person, personality and emotional maturity all have an impact on how abuse manifests itself. For example, exposure, which happened to me, may not seem as devastating as incest. But it still had an effect and should not be minimized or even denied. Stuffing it or saying, "it was no big deal" only makes it worse. Second, it was not my job to be their therapist. It was my job to be a wise friend, to treat each person and what happened to them with respect and compassion. God developed his compassion in me as I journeyed with these women.

I never knew why my experience kept cropping up. I minimized it since it was just "exposure." Being in this ministry made me face some of my own stuff and admit I had some control issues. I also came to realize that I struggle with trust issues. I do not freely grant my trust. Trust is earned and it takes a long time. Even though my husband and I were pastors, I can have struggles trusting God, too. Something which helps me trust God is this prayer practice:

I hold my hands out…palms up and say to God, "Here is what I am holding"
I turn my hands over, palms down and say," I let it go…help me trust You".

I saw much generational sin in that church and community. I talked about it with my mother, and also about that day I showed up with the horse on our doorstep. I remembered her calling the police while the horse ate up our grass in the backyard. My mother then shared with me that her father had molested her, and the behavior was passed down in the family. I was shocked. What? Our family? But we are Christians and go to church every Sunday! However, we are also broken human beings. It was a dark family secret and my mom decided it needed to end. She talked with us about what her father did and set up good boundaries to ensure we were not around him. She told me he also molested his son, my uncle, who is currently in jail for molesting his own children. Recently, I was able to talk about it with my aunts and a cousin who were also my grandfather's prey. Just talking about it, in a loving, safe environment was such a powerful healing experience for all of us. We agreed that just as generational sin is past down, the bondage can also be broken. Through "The Freedom in Christ" materials and ministry, God helped my mother break free from the bondage of generational sexual sin. Breaking free and forgiveness is a process…often life-long.

My psychologist told me that many men who are molested do molest their own children. The National Center for Victims of Crime states that most offenders are overwhelmingly male and that 60% of sexual abuse is by someone the person knows. This type of sin can be broken when just one person has the courage to speak up.

Identifying Control

Like Darla shared, many women are controlling in order to have a sense of security and stability in their lives. As children being abused, their lives were out of control. The more insecure we are, the more we try to control our environment, our circumstances and our relationships. This gives a warped sense of power or security and yet worry, anxiety, judgment, and negativity still reside inside. Reflecting on your control issues will help give insight as to what this is really all about.

Common Control Issues:

Everyone needs to do it my way, especially my grown kids.
I will never let anyone control me again.
I need to be right and what I say goes.
I need to be in charge.
I need to have the attention.
I don't need anyone in my life, especially someone telling me what to do.
If I hoard this money, this stuff, then I will be ok.
I am not eating so I can stay thin.
I have the solution to their problem and need to fix it.

Mark what you identify with.

Is there something not on this list that pertains to you?

_____

_____

What is God asking you to let go of and let Him?

_____

_____

Why do you struggle with letting go? What is your deeper need?

_____

_____

Offer yourself compassion for your deeper need that is not being met.

If you are a "control freak," or are codependent, I would suggest joining a support group, similar to a 12-step group. Give yourself compassion for the uncontrollable home life you were or are still in. Remember its ok to want the best for someone and not have them get hurt, however, give them the dignity to make and experience the consequences of their own decisions.

Codependency

Codependency is a term used to describe those who have been affected by difficult life circumstances. They try to control others or allow themselves to be controlled by others. They can feel responsible for the actions and feelings of others. The latter was true for me. I wanted to take responsibility for people's feelings. I liked it when people were happy but ran away when they were angry. I would take it personally as opposed to just letting people have whatever feelings they have. I had to learn not to try and "fix it." Now I am able to "hold" both positive and negative feelings in my own life and well as offer this "holding" to others.

Something that was life-changing for me was joining a small group for co-dependency. It helps to have community, to be heard, encouraged, have accountability and learn from one another. The workbook we went through was *Untangling Relationships: A Christian Perspective on Codependency* by Pat Springle.[13] There is so much to share and yet one thing that God revealed to me was:

When I step in to fix someone, I am not giving them the dignity to take charge of their own life and their relationship with God. I am interfering with what God is doing in their lives.

Taking responsibility for someone is not the same as teaching, encouraging or offering advice when asked. I will step in and say something if I think someone is going to cause harm or whose thinking is not based in reality. For example, if someone says she is not good enough, I will encourage her to replace lies with truth (Chapter Four). Or if someone is going to go tell someone off then I may encourage them to take a few breaths and pray about how best to confront them (Chapter Five).

"Holding" feelings is what I practice now. It means I accept both the positive and the negative feelings in my being. I don't ignore or stuff or deny the negative. In my own life, I will hold both fear or valid concern with hope in the same place. I also hold both joy and sadness together, gratitude for what is and disappointment for what is not. For example, I may be grateful for what a certain relationship offers and yet disappointed for what it does not. As a spiritual director, I offer this "Holding Feelings" to others. I allow them to express their anger, disappointment, sadness, etc. without trying to fix them or move to the positive too quickly. I am able to offer listening, encouragement, companionship, prayer and help that is appropriate. They are responsible for their own feelings and for their own relationship with God and others. They will go to God with their hurt, anger, or other feelings when they are ready.

Reflection

Who do you tend to control? _____

_____

What is that about? _____

_____

Who tries to control you? _____

_____

Why are you surrendering your power over to them? _____

_____

Whose feelings are you trying to take responsibility for? _____

_____

Who are you trying to rescue or enable? _____

_____

Why do you feel you need to rescue them? _____

_____

Or do you have a victim mentality and need to be rescued? _____

_____

Enabling is doing something for someone who can do this for themselves. How does this speak to you? _____

_____

Is this a true 911? A real Good Samaritan story? Or are you stepping to help when you should not? _____

_____

A Messiah complex is someone who thinks they have to save someone. Or someone can't do it without them or the ministry won't survive without them. Thoughts? Feelings?

_____

_____

As you reflect over what you wrote, ask what is God's responsibility? Ask what is theirs and what is mine?

Controlling God

Sometimes people try to control God whether they have experienced trauma or not. They put God in their box. Since God is infinite and not fully known, understood, or explained, then people may reject Him or put Him in a box. How can an infinite God who is all knowing, all powerful and everywhere in all things be fully known with our limited human brain?

I explain it by looking at the stars at night. I can see the moon, Big Dipper, Little Dipper and many twinkling starts. The most powerful telescope can see planets in our solar system and far away galaxies. Yet even that telescope is limited. There is so much more out there in the Universe we humans just can't see and know. And God created all that!

I also use the ocean as an analogy. As I stand on Sunset Cliffs, I can see the vast waters of Ocean Beach. The ocean reminds me of God in several ways. The ocean is so huge with what seems like a never-ending edge. I can see the powerful waves and hear the calming, peaceful sound they make. When it's summer, I can feel the water against my skin. Before the wave breaks, it can lift me up. I have respect for the strong currents and am mindful of the lifeguard's warning. There is such a joy playing and swimming in the ocean. Sometimes I can see some fish or a stingray on the ocean floor. I know there are many more sea creatures even though I cannot see them. As I watch the sunset, I am reminded how infinite God's love is for me. As the sun goes down, I offer gratitude for the blessings of my day and let go what of whatever I need to. I am still, quiet, peaceful. I do not notice the houses, distractions, street noise, people, problems that are behind me. Because my eyes are focused on the Son (sun).

The more I spend time with God, the more I know Him…the more I don't know Him.

I am ok with "Holding," both knowing God and not knowing God. I am limited, not all knowing, all present, all powerful, and yet I can experience God. My God is not in a box.

Another problem I have seen when people say, "God told me to tell you…" If God wants to tell you something, He can tell you Himself. Take what others say to God and then listen for yourself. Here are some questions for reflection.

o How do you put God in a box?
o How do you try to control God?
o How have others tried to control you by using God?
o How do you try to control others by using God

Centering Prayer

Psalm 46:10 tells us to "Be still and know I am God." Many of us have a hard time being still. And yet it's so important if we want to hear His voice. In our busy world, we are so distracted by work, texting, technology, Facebook, relationships, and more. Resting and being silent are becoming lost arts in our world. For many of us, when we are in solitude our thoughts are running like crazy in our heads. Often these thoughts can lead us down a negative, winding path. I have found centering prayer a wonderful tool for quieting my soul, learning to hear God's voice, and experiencing healing in my life.

For reading, I would suggest *Open Mind, Open Heart* by Thomas Keating.[14] He is a monk and also an alcoholic who has done many writings on centering prayer. This prayer helps with releasing control, with letting go and letting God. An organization called Contemplative Outreach has created centering prayer groups around the nation.

Centering prayer is a form of meditation. It is similar to contemplative prayer and silent prayer except the focus is on a sacred word. This can be done alone or within a group. The original instruction is to practice twice a day for 20 minutes. Some people do it once a day and may start with 10 minutes and slowly work up to 20 minutes. You can decide what works best for you.

- Find a quiet, safe place.
- Use a clock or timer so you can keep your eyes closed.
- Choose a sacred word, a name or attribute of God such as God, Jesus, Love, Joy, Comforter, Encourager, etc. and focus on that word. My favorite word was Healer.
- When other thoughts enter in (and they will) put them in an imaginary cupboard and tend to those thoughts later. Say your word, silently or out loud, and this will help you return your focus to Him.

Research has shown that meditation can change brain chemistry and bring about healing. There is research to support that this is true of Centering Prayer as well. Also, when I am focusing on Him, then I am not able to focus on any "stinking thinking." Journaling your experience and any insights can be an added benefit.

Serenity Prayer

"God, grant me the serenity to accept the things I cannot change, the courage to change what I can and the wisdom to know the difference between the two." AA and Al-Anon. [15]

This is a great prayer for releasing control. AA and Al-Anon tell their members that they cannot change people nor control what they choose to do. They stress living one day at a time. Jesus told people not to worry what to eat, drink, etc., and that each day had enough trouble of its own. Try reflecting on the serenity prayer. Like most repetitive prayers, it can become rote. Reflect on this prayer mindfully and ask only for what you need today.

"God" Who is God to you in this moment? _____

_____

_____

"grant me serenity" Name the kind of serenity you are looking for today (feeling of well-being, ability to trust, peace). _____

_____

_____

"to accept the things I cannot change" List what you cannot change today. _____

_____

_____

_____

"the courage to change what I can" What one thing can you change today? What is one step you can take today to change it? _____

_____

_____

_____

"the wisdom to know the difference." What wisdom do you need today? _____

_____

_____

_____

Model of Jesus

God created us with free will. Jesus did not control others. He offered eternal life, unconditional love, internal freedom and fulfilling relationship. Many chose to accept His gift while others did not.

Jesus invited the disciples and other people to follow Him (Mark 1:16-19). He didn't use force or manipulation.

Jesus sent out His followers to share the good news with others. "If you are not welcomed, not listened to, quietly withdraw. Don't make a scene. Shrug your shoulders and be on your way." (Mark 6:11 MSG) He didn't push.

Jesus had his core group of followers: the twelve disciples. He had many others such as the 72 (John 10). When they chose to leave, Jesus let them go. He didn't chase after people.

Jesus was not codependent. He did not enable people. He told people to take responsibility for their actions and allowed them to experience the consequences. He offered healing with compassion and then sent them home (Mark 8:26, 5:19, 2:11, 1:43-44).

Jesus allowed people, including us, to choose how we use our talents and gifts that God has given to us (Luke 19:11-27).

Jesus did not put God in a box of rules. Actually, He actually broke the box by healing on the Sabbath (Mark 3:1-6). In those days, and still today with Orthodox Jews, no work is to be done on the Sabbath, not even good work. When Jesus and his disciples were not fasting according to tradition (Mark 2:18-19), He did not allow the Pharisee's questioning to influence His decision. Jesus and His disciples picked grains of wheat on the Sabbath because they were hungry. Again, He broke the rule stating that the Sabbath was made for man, not man for the Sabbath (Mark 2:27). Many of the religious leaders of that time, the Pharisees, were more concerned about maintaining rules and traditions than helping those in need, meeting their own needs and listening to God's will in the moment.

Jesus surrendered control of His life over to God. He stated that He could do nothing by Himself, only what the Father is doing. Because the Father loved Him and showed Him all He does (John 5:19-20).

Jesus didn't try to control God in the garden. He asked God if there was any other way other than the cross. Yet He gave up His will, for God wanted Him to do (Mark 14:36). He trusted God with His pain and knew He would be with Him through it.

I encourage you to take an honest look at how you try to control yourself, others and even God. I understand that you need to feel safe and secure. The trauma you experienced left you with a feeling of fear, of life being out of control. God knows your wounded heart. He longs to melt your deepest fears, transforming them into faith, into peace, into love. All you need to do is let go of your control and open your heart to Him.

He is waiting with open arms.

Chapter Eight
Worry and Anxiety

I have worried about many things in my life. Most of which never happened.
— Mark Twain[16]

Worry does not empty tomorrow of its troubles; it empties today of its strength.
— Corrie Ten Boom[17]

Therefore, do not worry about tomorrow, for tomorrow will worry about itself. Each day has enough trouble of its own.
— Jesus Christ

We all struggle with worry and anxiety. Not knowing what will happen is a hard place to be. Some of us have that "spinning Ferris wheel" in our heads more than others. This often leads to trying to control a situation or others. Or we worry about it, believing that will help the situation. Both of these are a waste of time and a drain on energy. Worry and anxiety can rob us of peace, joy, and freedom.

Common Worry and Anxiety:

What is going to happen to me?
What is going to happen to my loved one?
Will I be taken care of?
Will I have enough money?
Will I have my health?
How am I going to deal with this?
What are they thinking of me?
I am not going to get love, a promotion, security, etc.

Reflection

Sit with God in silence. Ask for wisdom. Reflect on the following questions:

What are you worrying about?   What is the video playing in your head? _____
_____
_____
_____

Why are you worried about this? _____
_____
_____

What is your deeper need? _____
_____
_____

What are your anxious thoughts? _____
_____
_____

What is causing these thoughts? _____
_____
_____

As Mark Twain said, most of his worries never happened. Do you know if your worries will happen? In other words, is this video playing in your head true? _____
_____
_____

Corrie Ten Boom stated that worry empties us of today's strength. Where is this happening in your life? What strength do you need today? _____
_____
_____

As Jesus Christ said, each day has enough trouble of its own. What is troubling you today? Talk to Jesus about it as you would a friend. _____
_____
_____

What is Jesus saying to you? _____
_____

I was 12 years old. In the middle of the night I was awakened by a noise outside my window. I felt nervous and afraid so I went into my mother's and stepfather's room. I tried to wake my stepfather and he told me to crawl in bed with him. Soon after getting in bed with him he began to fondle me, first my breasts and then lower. I was confused and didn't understand what was happening. This didn't feel right. I wondered if he thought I was my mom. I know I was confused. Although I didn't have language for it then, I felt violated and probably some of level of fear began to take root.

I told my mother the next day. She didn't react much, but she did confront him. He talked to me in her presence and his demeanor seemed very remorseful. He apologized to me.

He and my mother were married when I was 5 years old. From the beginning he was never affectionate, paternal, nurturing or loving with me or his own biological children. Their marriage was a great struggle, with drinking, gambling and financial issues. When I was 13, he went to prison for writing bad checks. After that, my mother, siblings and I moved. My mom managed without him and life was peaceful for a year. At the end of that year he was released from prison and came back home. I can remember feeling so disappointed, discouraged, and resentful. Because of his record and poor credit, he wanted to move out of state for a new beginning. He was quite a charmer and con man. Things were always going to be better, according to him. The problem was, they never were.

One evening he got drunk, they fought, and he hit my mother. I was 13 at the time, and my siblings and I were in bed. I heard him hit her and then he left the apartment. I got out of bed, turned the hall light on and saw my mother at the bottom of the stairs. I ran down the stairs to her, saw that she was bleeding from some kind of head wound and was unconscious. I was so scared. I called my uncle who called for an ambulance. I sat at the bottom of the stairs with my mother when my stepfather returned home. Anger welled up inside me. I screamed at him to get out!

While my mother was in the hospital, I was responsible for getting my younger siblings and myself ready for school. I also took care of laundry and other household things. I developed a codependency of warped responsibility towards my mother and siblings. Then my stepfather, who was back at home, began to make advances towards me. I was overwhelmed with fear, anxiety and all the responsibilities. I was constantly looking around to see if I was safe or if I needed to dodge his wayward advances. I had no one to comfort, help, or protect me. Home was not at all safe.

I needed to get out of the mess. At 18, I moved out. My mother went ballistic and yelled all kinds of accusations at me. I had always hoped we could be a loving, stable and safe family. Sadly, this desire never came true.

I developed bitter root judgments toward my mother and stepfather. I judged them for being poor parents, not safe, not dependable, not trustworthy and a whole lot more. I had so much resentment, anger, bitterness, and judgment towards my stepfather. He was also an emotionally unavailable man. I ended up marrying someone who was also emotionally unavailable.

I had definitely been victimized but also developed a victim mentality. Growing up I struggled with so much shame and embarrassment because of the fallout of my stepfather's bad choices. I also struggled with guilt and shame when I became sexually active. In my first sexual experience, I was hoping for intimacy and oneness. Sadly, it wasn't to be found in that relationship. I married in my mid-twenties. My husband-to-be was not very sensitive to my sexual issues resulting from my stepfather's molestation and my own unhealthy choices. I struggled with resentment towards my husband for his lack of respect for my boundaries in this area. I was also angry at myself for not being strong enough to say no, as I was too afraid of rejection. I had difficulty knowing how to take care of myself, ask for what I needed and set boundaries.

Over the years, I have grown and God has done significant healing in my life, especially through Healing Prayer. I have more confidence and freedom to enjoy my sexuality. My fear of men has diminished significantly. I am able to set appropriate boundaries and have discovered I have a voice.

Healing Prayer creates space for the power of the Holy Spirit to reveal any lies one believes, to denounce any strongholds such as a bitter root judgment, receiving forgiveness, power and healing. I was so grateful for this experience that I went into training for Sozo Healing Prayer. I have been able to journey with hundreds of men and women who desire this internal freedom in all aspects of their lives.

God is definitely my Healer!

Spiritual Practices and Prayers

Four Breaths a Minute

This is used by many therapists. I find it helpful to focus on an image of God while I do this. Inhale slowly on the count of 7 and exhale on the count of 8, taking 4 breaths in one minute. Try this for several minutes. This is useful when in a suddenly stressful setting that causes anxiety. Excuse yourself to the bathroom, close the door and just sit and breathe. Or in the middle of night, when you wake up and feel anxious, just focus on God and breathe.

Contemplative Prayer

Any of the previous silent prayers, such as Centering Prayer or Soaking Prayer, help with worry and anxiety.

Meditation

Meditation on scripture or a saying such as *All Shall be Well* (Julian of Norwich)[18] or *One day at a time* (AA) can be helpful. One of my favorite passages is Luke 12: 22-31.

> Then Jesus said to his disciples: "Therefore I tell you, do not worry about your life, what you will eat; or about your body, what you will wear. Life is more than food, and the body more than clothes. Consider the ravens.: they do not sow or reap, they have no storeroom or barn; yet God feeds them. *And how much more valuable you are than birds!* Who of you by worrying can add a single hour to his life? Since you cannot do this very little thing, why do you worry about the rest?
>
> Consider how the lilies grow. They do not labor or spin. Yet I tell you, not even Solomon in all his splendor was dressed like one of these. If that is how God clothes the grass of the field, which is here today, and tomorrow is thrown into the fire, how much more will He clothe you, O you of little faith! And do not set your heart on what you will eat or drink; do not worry about it. For the pagan world runs after all such things, and your Father knows that you need them. But seek his kingdom and these things will be given to you as well.
>
> Luke 12:22-31 (NIV)

Try Lectio Divina. Read the passage out loud, slowly, 3 times. What jumps out at you in the passage?

- How does this passage relate to your life?
- What is Jesus saying to you?
- Meditate on this or a portion of this passage.

Internal Fasting

I remember the first time the letter came in the mail to me from the radiology department regarding the results of my mammogram. The words jumped off the page: THE RESULTS WERE ABNORMAL. The tune playing in my head was *what if*? What if it is cancer? What am I going to do? I suddenly went down the road to doom and had my funeral all planned out. I went back in for an ultrasound and the doctor said it was a cyst. No worries. See you next year.

What a waste of time and energy.

Even in small things, I can read more into situations than was intended. One area is with e-mail. I say to others (and to myself) not to send any kind of confrontation in text or an e-mail. So much can be misunderstood since there is no body language, no warm facial expressions and no tone of voice. Sometimes I have made false assumptions as to what someone meant and was way off base. At other times, I have been misunderstood and wondered what I said wrong. Of course, the ideal is to talk it through with someone to clarify what they truly meant and vice versa. Sometimes I can go down that spiraling path that leads to nowhere, but a lot of headaches and precious time lost for me. I could have been dwelling on what is true, not this made-up, damaging scenario in my head.

Another example is when well-intentioned people, especially leaders, say you should be doing this or that. Or this kind of prayer practice is the best. Or this kind of service is the best. Well, it may be their belief or opinion and not what God has for me. We tend to feel our way is the best way for everyone else, too.

One year, during Lent, I decided to do what I call internal fasting. Instead of giving up chocolate or food or wine, I chose to give up grave digging, shopping the future and making false assumptions.

Grave Digging

I first heard this from Joe McHugh, SJ. [19]He said there is no life in a grave, only bones and decay. Since then I have been able to put this into practice as well as share it with others.

- What in the past are you ruminating on? What is that video from the past that keeps playing over and over again?
- Is there something that stills needs to be worked through?
- Have you grieved over the loss? (Chapter 11)
- Have you forgiven or received forgiveness? (Chapter 12)
- How can you press an imaginary delete button?

Shopping the Future

I heard this phrase, *"Don't shop the future"*, from a friend of mine, Karen Lenell[20], who is a retired MFT. We don't know what will happen tomorrow. No one knows what the future will bring. Worrying about the future is wasted time and energy.

- What are you shopping for?
- If it's not good, take this back to the store, get a receipt and go home. In other words, take it to God if you have a valid concern. Its ok to "hold" the situation with God. For example, it's normal to be concerned about an abnormal mammogram. I can "hold" my concern with God while not going down the planning-my-funeral scenario.

Stop Making Assumptions

I have gotten in trouble by making false assumptions. I have done this to others and others have done this to me.

- Ask yourself is this really true? Do I have the facts? Is there proof?
- Did this person really say this? Or intend this?
- According to whom? Is this according to God or according to a person?
- STOP making a scenario. **If don't know…let it go.**

Philippians Chapter Four

The next worksheet is based on Philippians, Chapter 4. This is a wonderful passage to contemplate on as Paul discusses four main human issues and how to surrender and trust God. The four main themes are: holding a grudge, worry and anxiety, lack of contentment and envy, and courage or strength.

> My dear, dear friends! I love you so much. I do want the very best for you. You make me feel such joy, fill me with such pride. Don't waver. Stay on track, steady in God.
> Philippians 4:1 (MSG)

Who in your life gives makes you feel such joy? Who truly wants the best for you? _____
_____
_____

Take a moment to express gratitude to God for this person (or people.)

> I urge Eudia and Syntyche to iron out their differences and make up. God doesn't want his children holding grudges.
> Philippians 4:2 (MSG)

Who are you holding a grudge against? How did they hurt you? Talk to God how you feel about it. _____
_____
_____

Ask God to help you begin the process of forgiveness (Chapter 12).

> Celebrate God all day, every day. I mean, revel in Him! Make it as clear to all you meet that you're on their side, working with them and not against them. Help them see that the Master is about to arrive. He could show up any minute!
> Philippians 4:4-5 (MSG)

Take a moment to celebrate what God has done for you in your life. Celebrate who He is.

> Don't fret or worry. Instead of worrying, pray. Let petitions and praises shape your worries into prayers, letting God know your concerns. Before you know it, a sense of God's wholeness, everything coming together for good, will come and settle you down. It's wonderful what happens when Christ displaces worry at the center of your life.
> Philippians 4:6-7 (MSG)

What are you worrying about now? _____

Talk to God about all your concerns. Be truly honest with Him about how you really feel.

_____

_____

Take these worries and concerns to God in prayer now. Sit with Him. Feel His gentle touch and His lavish love. He accepts you just as you are . . . worries, concerns and all.

What is He saying to you about your worries and concerns? _____

_____

_____

> Summing it all up, friends, I'd say you'll do best by filling your minds and meditation on things true, noble, reputable, authentic, compelling, gracious, the best...not the worst; the beautiful, not the ugly, things to praise, not things to curse. Put into practice what you have learned from me, what you heard and saw and realized. Do that, and God, who makes everything work together will work you into His most excellent harmonies.
> Philippians 4:8-9 (MSG)

Name something true about God, maybe a characteristic or a promise. _____

_____

_____

_____

What is something noble? _____

_____

Reputable? _____

_____

What is authentic? About you? About God? _____

_____

_____

_____

Sometimes we worry about things that haven't happened or may not even happen.
Sometimes we believe a lie from the evil one or from someone who has been hurtful to us.

> In everything, with Thanksgiving, make your requests known to God
> Philippians 4:6 (NIV)

131

Ask yourself:

Is it true? Am I really going to lose my house? Am I really an insignificant person? Can I really trust God and let go of my control? _____

_____

_____

What are you grateful for? _____

_____

_____

Look at your difficult situation. Name the worst about it. What is the best about it? What is He teaching you in this? Where is He leading you? _____

_____

_____

What is beautiful about your life? _____

_____

_____

What would you like to praise God for? _____

_____

_____

> Do that, and God, who makes everything work together, will work for you into His most excellent harmonies.
>
> Philippians 4:9 (MSG)

What is the "do that" in your life? What is Jesus inviting you into? _____

_____

_____

Do you believe God will work everything together for you? Why or why not? _____

_____

_____

Can you recall a time where God worked something out in your life? _____

_____

_____

How can this help you trust God with your current situation?

_____

_____

_____

> I'm glad in God, far happier than you would ever guess…happy that you are again showing such strong concern for me. Not that you ever quit praying and thinking about me. You just had no chance to show it.
>
> Philippians 4:10-14 (MSG)

Do you have someone in your life that prays with you and can come along side you? If yes, spend some time in Thanksgiving for this person(s). _____

_____

Who do you show concern for?_____

_____

> Actually, I don't have a sense of needing anything personally. I have learned by now to be quite content whatever my circumstances. I am just as happy with little as with much, with much as with little. I have found the recipe for being happy whether full or hungry, hands full or hands empty.
>
> Philippians 4:11-12 (MSG)

Circle the areas of Contentment in your life.   Draw a square around the areas of Discontent.

Money   Possessions   House

Relationships: parents spouse friends children   relatives   co-workers   myself other

Self: body   health   talents   personality   emotional health   other

God: His timing   His ways   feeling His presence   unanswered prayers   other

Job: success   security   conflict   policies   lack of interest   money

Church: the leaders   the service   community   teachings   programs other

"True contentment is wanting what I have."   Neil Anderson

Look at the areas you are content with. Express gratitude for being content.

_____

_____

_____

Now look at the areas you are discontent with. Ask yourself without judgment: What is my desire in this area? What do I really wish I had? _____

_____

_____

What are my deeper needs? (Security, belonging, being loved, heard, understood, respected or valued, feeling worthy or significant, having hope, etc.) _____

_____

_____

The opposite of contentment is envy. Where does envy show up in my life? _____

_____

_____

How can I learn to be content with the things I have?_____

_____

_____

How can I learn to be content with the relationships I have or more content with being alone with myself?_____

_____

What will help me "wait" on God while I am wanting something? _____

_____

_____

Prayer practice

- Spend time reading Paul's description of the body and how we all have unique gifts in 1 Corinthians 12:12-31.
- Identify what part of the body you are. Search your heart for any lack of contentment with the part you are or the part you used to be.
- Express gratitude for who you are and what you have been given.
- Search your heart for any comparison or envy of someone else's part. Ask God to help you stop comparing yourself to another as this leads to envy and jealousy and ultimately lack of contentment.
- Rejoice in this truth: there is only one you!

Prayer: Lord God I thank you that I am a _____ in the body of Christ. Help me be content with what I have been given and how you have created me. Help me be grateful for what I do have. Help me release to you my negative thoughts on what I do not have. Replace any feelings of jealously and envy with being truly happy for others when they are blessed. As Paul learned, help me also learn to be content with many or few, little or much. Help me serve you with the gifts I have. I rejoice for there is only one me! Amen.

> I can do everything through Him who gives me strength.
> Philippians 4:13 (NIV)
> Whatever I have, wherever I am, I can make it through anything in the One who makes me who I am.
> Philippians 4:13 (MSG)

Where in your life do you need to ask God for strength? _____
_____
_____

Where or with what in your life do you need to step out and take courage? _____
_____
_____

What is holding you back? _____
_____
_____

What prayer practice will help you trust God to give you the strength and courage you need to get through your situation/circumstance? _____
_____
_____

Take a few moments with your practice and go to God in silence.

> I don't mean that your help didn't mean a lot to me—it did. It was a beautiful thing that you came alongside me in my troubles.
> Philippians 4:14-17 (MSG)

Who can you count on to come alongside you in your troubles? Who can count on you?
_____
_____

> You Philippians well know, and you can be sure I will never forget it, that when I first left Macedonia province, venturing out with the Message, not one church helped out in the give-and-take of this work except you. You were the only one. Even while I was in Thessalonica, you helped out—and not only once, but twice. Not that I am looking for handouts, but I do want you to experience the blessing that issues from generosity.
>
> Philippians 4:15-17 (MSG)

What does give and take in a relationship look like to you? _____
_____
_____
_____

How do you practice generosity? _____
_____
_____
_____

In summary, you are not alone in your worry or anxiety. Spend time with God, talk to Him like you would a friend about your worries. He wants to listen to your heart. He does not judge you. Sometimes just being able to share without having someone judge me can be a such a relief.

Try not to go grave digging. There is no life there, only decay. Shopping the future will only bring disappointment and robs you of strength you need for today. When you start to make an assumption, ask yourself if this is true. If you don't know then choose not to go down that made-up-scenario-destructive-road. Your time and your internal state of well-being are far more valuable than that. Instead, "hold" your valid concern before God. Breathe deeply, meditate, or say a brief prayer.

Philippians Four is great advice and encouragement for everyday living. Remember to give your requests to God along with thanksgiving. He is concerned with what you are concerned about. He will give you the strength you need to get through the day. Learn to be content and offer yourself some grace when you slip into envy and discontentment. I don't know how the apostle Paul did it when he practiced joy in prison after he had been whipped and was waiting on death row. If he can learn to be content, so can we.

Jesus tells us in Luke 12:22 to look at how God cares for birds. They have food, a tree for shelter, feathers for warmth. And He says we are far more valuable than the birds. He encourages us to remember that God will take care of us and that worry cannot add a single hour to our life. You and I are truly are valuable to Him. We are like beautiful sparrows.

Chapter Nine
Idolatry and Addictions

Pamela: *I numbed myself with shopping. I bought things to fill that hole inside. I would drop my daughter off at school every day and then go to the mall.*

Maddison: *I developed a shopping addiction and lived at Nordstrom.*

Amber: *I became codependent and ended up in Al-Anon. I needed to be successful and was driven to be on top.*

Clara: *I developed a codependency of being responsible for other people. A bitter root judgment lived in my heart.*

Missy: *I became addicted to sex.*

Nancy: *I filled that empty place with work. I was driven to be successful.*

Darla: *I saw so many women who were abused become control freaks. I, too, have an issue with control.*

Jane: *I struggled with control and codependency of my grown children.*

I became obsessed with my weight and struggled with my body image. I also tried to fill that hole with success and relationships.

Trauma creates a hole, a wound in us. Almost every wounded soul I know, including myself, tries to fill it with something or someone.

We truly do have a gracious God. He longs to come into our deepest wound, clean out the "pus" and fill it with His unending love. When we begin to see and admit what we fill that hole with, then we can begin the process of replacing our idol with His love. And He is more than willing to help us become free and whole and content.

I hope you are beginning to know and feel in your heart that He loves you and accepts you just as you are, just where you are right now. Scripture tells us that the greatest commandment is to love God with our whole heart, mind and soul. (Wow... this is difficult!) He asks us to have no idols above Him. He wants us to desire Him more than anyone or anything else. Many of us think that we are ok if we don't worship a statue or golden calf. Most of us are unaware of our idols, which I define as anything that is more important than God.

In this chapter, I hope you will explore what gets in the way of loving God with your whole heart, mind and soul. Letting go of what we are getting our identity in is hard work. See this as a positive exercise: a way of drawing closer and deeper with God. He does not condemn or criticize you. He will help you let go of what you are filling that void with. Only God can truly satisfy and fill your soul.

Idolatry

God created us for relationship with Him. Genesis tells us we are created in His image. Psalm 139:13-14 tells us we are fearfully and wonderfully made. Romans 8:38-39 tells us nothing can separate us from His love. Jeremiah 29:11 says He has a plan for us. Isaiah 43:5 tells us we are precious to Him. Ephesians 2:10 states we are His masterpiece. Sometimes we have a hard time believing all this is true and relevant for us today. We struggle with trusting God and His love for us. We tend to pursue something else or someone else instead, often we are not even aware of this.

Jesus tells us that the greatest commandment is to love God with our whole mind, heart and soul (Matt.22:37). Wow…this is not easy! Most of us raised in the church would nod our head in agreement while deep down struggling with loving God first in our lives. I was blind to some of my idols until God got my attention. Although it was a difficult time in my life, I became aware of what I loved more than God. I didn't worship golden calves but I did get my value from success.

In my early career, I worked at a school for the deaf and hard of hearing. I enjoyed helping them learn how to speak and hear through amplification. Later, I entered the business world in a related field and eventually got caught up in the "numbers" game. I wanted to be so successful in my job that I was too driven. My boss was thrilled and my ego became inflated. Scripture tells us in the Parable of the Talents that the servants who invested their master's money and made a profit were rewarded while the servant who did nothing was punished. Throughout the book of Proverbs, hard work is encouraged and blessed by God. It truly is a good thing to do the best job you can.

The problem for me was that success became my identity and my relationship with God was nil. It was like being married to someone and just living together, sleeping in a separate bed and never talking. Even though I was successful, I was lonely and knew there was something missing. So I retired and started a ministry in a church. I told myself that I would go work for God. Again, I was driven—this time to build a big and successful women's mentoring ministry. Nothing really changed.

It was the same idol, different venue.

Then, after my friend's verbal confrontation — an attack that triggered buried issues — I needed to step out of ministry for a season. I entered into a deeper place with God and spent much time alone with Him. He wanted me to get my identity in Him. I didn't need to work for His approval as He already loved me just as I was. I desired to re-connect with my first love. From that place of being the beloved, I entered back into ministry as a spiritual director. I have let go of needing to be successful. I genuinely desire to come alongside women who have been wounded emotionally and encourage them to connect with their first love: God. I have learned to be content with many or with few.

Sadly, I see many well-intentioned priests, pastors, and ministry leaders enter the ministry with genuine desire to serve God and help others. Then the ego creeps in and they may get caught up in the numbers game: attendance, money, approval or recognition from others. These things are good, actually a part of human reality. What I am saying is to be the best, do the best with what God has called you to, while loving Him first in your heart, mind and body.

A prayer I say is: *God, help me think not too highly or not too lowly of myself.*

Another idol was to get my identity in what others thought of me and their approval. God showed me He wants me to get my identity in Christ, in who He says I am. This, too, has been a lifelong process. As I have spent time with Him, allowing Him to "fill" me, I am freer. I don't take things personally like I used to. I am grateful for who I am, accepting both my talents and my flaws. I am working on accepting people for who they are, not how they approve or disapprove of me.

Do you long for more intimacy with God? To desire Him above all else? Then take a deep breath and ask for wisdom as to what competes in your heart, soul, mind and strength for God. Before you explore your idols, please know that loving God first with every part of your being is not easy. Our desire ought to be more of God and less of the idols we are attached to. Letting go of our idols takes time. Remember He loves you and accepts you where you are. He longs for intimacy and wants to be first in your heart. Be willing to take an honest look at what pulls your time, your thoughts, your attention and your affection away from spending more time with Him. As we are filled with His love, we will be able to love ourselves and others from a place of being the Beloved as opposed to a desperate, false sense of fulfillment.

Most people get their self-worth from the 3 P's: Power, Prestige and Possessions. Another way of putting it is: money, success or relationships. Let's look at some famous scripture passages.

> Money: "Do not store up for yourselves treasure on earth, where moth and rust destroy, and where thieves break in and steal. But store up for yourselves treasures in heaven, where moth and rust do not destroy and where thieves do not break in and steal. For where your treasure is, there your heart will be also."
> Matthew 6:19
>
> Relationships: "Anyone who loves his father or mother more than me is not worthy of me, anyone who loves his son or daughter more than me is not worthy of me, and anyone who does not take up his cross and follow me is not worthy of me."
> Matthew 10:37
>
> Success: At that time, the disciples came to Jesus and asked, "Who is the greatest in the kingdom of heaven?" He called a little child and had him stand among them. And he said, "I tell you the truth, whoever humbles himself like this child is the greatest in the kingdom of heaven."
> Matthew 18:1
>
> "Everything they do (religious leaders at that time) is done for man to see."
> Matthew 23:5

Jesus probably will not ask you to give up all your possessions, your family and your success. I believe He will want these things to not become obsessions or more important than him. Balance is important. He may ask you to spend a little less time in some area, so you can spend more time with Him. On the other hand, if you are partaking in something harmful, such as a substance addiction, you will need to give that up and seek professional help.

On the next page is an Imaginative Prayer practice on the Rich Young Ruler. Read the scripture slowly three times. Then put yourself in the passage and answer the questions that follow the scripture.

> Now a man came up to Jesus and asked, "Teacher, what good thing must I do to get eternal life?"
>
> "Why do you ask me about what is good?" Jesus replied, "There is only One who is good. If you want to enter life, obey the commandments."
>
> "Which ones?" the man inquired.
>
> Jesus replied, "Do not murder, do not commit adultery, do not steal, do not give false testimony, honor your father and mother and love your neighbor as yourself."
>
> "All these I have kept," the young man said, "What do I still lack?"
>
> Jesus answered, "If you want to be perfect, go sell your possessions and give to the poor and you will have treasure in heaven. Then come, follow me."
>
> When the young man heard this, he went away sad, because he had great wealth.
>
> Matthew 19:16

Imagine you are in this scene.

- What do you see? What do you hear?
- What do you feel as you listen to this conversation?
- What is stirring inside you as Jesus talks about the greatest commandments?
- What is your response when you hear what Jesus said this young man lacked?
- How do you feel when he walked away?

> Jesus looked at him and loved him.   Mark 10:21

Now you are the young man or woman. You have come to find Jesus. You love Him and genuinely want to follow him with your whole heart, mind and soul. You have tried to follow the commandments. Imagine Him gazing at you with love.

- What does that feel like?
- Come and sit with Him. Don't be afraid. When you are ready, ask Him honestly:
- What do I lack?
- What do I love more than You?
- What do I need to let go of so I have more time with You?
- Listen to His voice.
- Journal your insights.

Exploring Your Idols

Sit with God in silence and solitude. Ask Him for wisdom and insight. Be real and authentic. He does not judge you. Read through the list below.

- What on this list competes with your love for God and spending time with Him?
- Put a check by those that apply. If you are not sure, ask a spouse or close friend to look at this list with you.
- What do you think about all the time?
- What do you fantasize about?
- What "video" is playing in your head?
- Where do you spend most of your time?

food	computer	codependency	success
alcohol	Facebook	worry	anger
drugs	smart phone	anxiety	regrets
smoking	X-box/video games	phobias	revenge
shopping	telephone	recognition	fame
exercise	technology	relationships	prestige
body image	television	resentment	power
sex	approval	possessions	jealousy/envy
masturbation	pornography	security	victim mentality
reading novels/magazines		money	animals
the need to be in control		environment	politics
the need to be effective		comparison	shame
the need to be right		control issues with _____	
the need to be the center of attention		overworking in church	
the need to live through your children		perfectionism	
control issues with children, minor or grown			other

The Idol of Body Image

A real problem is our society is poor body image, especially among women. This is especially true of women who have been abused. Our culture worships outer appearance and beauty. Women are told by the media to look like supermodels. Being thin is "in." We women struggle with feeling insecure about our weight, our height, our hair, our skin, etc. This doesn't mean we should not take care of ourselves in a healthy way. It means we need to become aware of and stop any obsessing over our bodies.

Food is an issue too in our culture. I know many women who use food to fill the hole inside created by their wounds. Other women have shared that since their childhood was out of control, the only thing they could control was how much or how little they ate. Scripture tells us everything God creates is good and is to be used in moderation. Abusing our bodies, whether it is with food, alcohol, substances, or "stinking thinking" (shame) is not a healthy way to love ourselves.

Karen Ritter, LCSW, had a private practice specializing in counseling women with eating disorders.[21] She commented that there is this notion that we should artificially control the size and appearance of our bodies with excessive dieting and exercise to comply with the cultural definition of how we are supposed to look. Instead, we need to trust our bodies to work as God created them while practicing moderation and listening to our hunger and fullness signals. Emotional, mindless eating abuses our bodies, as does excessive and compulsive exercise. She recommends the book *The Religion of Thinness* by Michelle M. Lelwica, ThD.[22]

I struggled with my body image most of my life. I can remember when I was in seventh grade, my mom made a comment my rear end was getting a little too big. I remember exactly what I was wearing and how hurt I felt. Also, I recall Mrs. Berger took a picture of Lindsey and me in the bathtub. We were around nine years old. I was tan from swimming. Mrs. Berger showed me the picture, laughing and saying, "Look at your big, fat white butt." I laughed along with her, yet inside I was hurting. From then on, I had an issue with my body and was constantly on a diet. I had a boyfriend in college who was obsessed with me being thin and wanted me to look like a super model. I also had some girlfriends who were obsessive about being thin. I wasn't aware that weight had become an idol for me until I went to a lecture at a seminary on body image. The woman who spoke was an MFT (marriage and family therapist). She stated it is unhealthy to be too overweight as well as too underweight. Both the food and weight loss industries are big money makers and play to our psyche in their advertising. She looked at us in the eye, saying that when we women don't accept our bodies, we are *dissing* (disrespecting) God, since He created us in His image. I was convicted! I wrote a letter to God, apologizing for the ways I "dissed" my body. I don't diet anymore. I try to eat healthy foods and exercise regularly. And I certainly don't dwell on it like I used to. I don't get on the scale every day. Since then, I have been able to accept my body, curves and all.

Scripture tells us in Genesis 1:27 that we are created in His image. The human body, both male and female, is created unique, beautiful, and in His image.

Body Image Exercise

I adapted this from Mark Gungor, pastor, speaker, and creator of *Laugh Your Way To a Better Marriage*. [23] He commented that many women in our society struggle with body image. Very few women in the world are super models and most of the pictures are air brushed. Studies have shown that Caucasian women, especially those in California, struggle more with their body image than African American or Hispanic women. He stated that most men don't care as much as women think they do about perfect bodies; they just want us to show up! He discussed body image using this passage:

Read Song of Songs 7:1-6 and 4:2. Solomon was describing this woman he loved.

Your hair is like a flock of goats......................................(bad hair day?)

How beautiful your sandaled feet ....(he really liked her feet)

Your graceful legs are like jewels ....(she had really nice legs)

Your navel is a rounded goblet...(she had an "outie")

Your waist is a mound of wheat...(ok, ladies . . . she had a tummy on her!)

Your breasts are like two fawns..(fawns are small)

Your neck is like an ivory tower ....(she had a very long neck)

Your eyes are like pools of Heshbon.................................(she had pretty eyes like water)

Your nose is like the tower of Lebanon ....(she had a big nose!)

Your head crowns you like Mount Carmel ....(she had a huge head!)

How beautiful you are and how pleasing! ....(he loved and accepted her)

Solomon was in love with this woman. He accepted her body and called her beautiful.

This is how God sees each one of us. Pastor Gungor stated that most men don't care if we are not a supermodel. Most men love a woman's body and really want her to be "present" and feel good in her own skin. I am grateful my husband feels this way about me. *I feel sorrow if you have a spouse or partner that pressures you to be thin.* Those hurtful words from my childhood along with the pressure from our culture that "thin is in" kept me from truly embracing my beautiful body, with my tower of Lebanon and mound of wheat!

Reflection

What did you learn about your body image growing up? From your parents? Peers?
Others? From Media? _____

_____

_____

_____

_____

Describe Your Body. _____

_____

_____

_____

_____

What do you like about it? _____

_____

_____

_____

_____

What do you criticize? _____

_____

_____

_____

_____

If you do struggle, do you know where this struggle comes from? Sit in silence with God
and ask Him to reveal this to you. _____

_____

_____

_____

_____

- If you have "dissed" your body, write a letter an apology letter to God.
- Then write an apology letter to your body.
- Embrace your unique feminine design!

If you do struggle with an eating disorder, such as anorexia, bulimia, or binge eating, please seek professional help. Eating disorders are very dangerous.

Healthy Sexuality

Missy: *I don't feel shame for my past as I know I am forgiven. Having said that, being sexually promiscuous--sleeping with over a hundred different men--has its ramifications that I will have to deal with the rest of my life.*

Maddison: *I felt shame because it felt good. I had to learn that our bodies were designed for pleasure and that is a good thing, not the abuse itself.*

Clara: *I was hoping for intimacy and oneness during sex which was lacking. My husband didn't respect my sexual issues which resulted from the molestation.*

Pamela: *I hated sex.*

Sex is more than genital stimulation and muscle contractions. It's more interesting than that. It's about intimacy, communication, pleasure in your body, feeling good and fun.

Laura Davis
Co-author of The Courage to Heal[24]

Our sexuality is such a God-given, integral aspect of our human experience, our sexuality deserves to be respected as a gift. And at the very minimum it means really then that our sexual boundaries be respected, namely that no one be sexual with us unless we want them to, that is through free consent between two adults as a free act of intimacy between two people who care about fulfillment that moves toward commitment, that makes the world go around, that is the foundation of the family. And so there is nothing that's more powerful at contributing to happiness and fulfillment as sexuality, in this broad sense of the world, but also, for that very reason because it's so intimate, nothing more destructive when it's abused or violated.

James Finley, PhD
Author of the article Standing Against Sexual Harassment and the Abuse of Power[25]

God created us, male and female, in His image. He created our sexuality and the act of sex as a beautiful gift to be shared in a committed relationship. This is a topic that many of us in the church shy away from talking about. Sometimes the media focuses on sex and sexuality too much or in a distorted way. Pornography often creates problems in intimacy within a committed relationship. Sexual abuse can affect one's view of their sexuality. On the next page are some questions to reflect on as you sit with God during your silent time. If you are comfortable, you may want to discuss some of these during your group time.

How were you taught about sex growing up? _____

_____

_____

_____

What are your thoughts and feelings towards sex? _____

_____

_____

_____

What are your feelings about your sexuality? _____

_____

_____

_____

How do you feel about your body? _____

_____

_____

_____

How do you feel that your body was made to experience pleasure? _____

_____

_____

_____

Are you able to experience pleasure with your spouse? Why or why not? ____

_____

_____

_____

Are you able to discuss your needs to your spouse, especially sexual needs? ___

_____

_____

_____

What do you need to feel sexual? What do you desire? _____

_____

_____

_____

What is your belief about masturbation? _____

_____

_____

_____

What are your thoughts about pornography? _____

_____

_____

What are your spouse's beliefs? _____

_____

_____

What sexual practices are ok for you and what are not? _____

_____

_____

_____

What boundaries will you set? _____

_____

_____

_____

How can you experience sensual experiences when you are alone? (e.g. a hot bath, a
massage, chocolate dipped strawberries, etc.). _____

_____

_____

How did the abuse affect your thoughts about sex, sexuality and body image? _____

_____

_____

_____

What steps can you take towards healing/repair? What is God inviting you into? _____

_____

_____

_____

   If you feel like you need healing in the area of sexuality, I would suggest finding a good
therapist. Several women I have journeyed with who suffered sexual abuse still struggled
with physical intimacy, even touch or a hug. Since trauma can get trapped in the body, some
have found help with EMDR or Trauma Therapy. I have seen a difference in them. There is
hope out there.

It takes tremendous courage to look inside and see what truly competes in your heart, your soul, your mind and your body for first place with God. Jesus challenged people to see their idols, to see what truly held them back from following Him. He did this because He loved them and wanted to have a closer relationship. I know I don't want my earthly husband to put another woman above me. Or a substance like alcohol. Or activities like a career or his work. All those things hold us back from being intimate physically, emotionally and spiritually. I can understand how God feels the same when we love something or someone more than Him.

I was so humbled when my wound was opened, and God slowly begin the process of healing and transformation. I had to come to that place where I admitted I often loved people and success more than Him. I am grateful for His grace every day and I ask Him to help me not let anything or anyone grow more important than Him. It's a daily challenge. When I fall, He is there to draw me back to Him.

The internal fruit of the Spirit is freedom to be who I am created to be! The freedom to serve my call and my purpose, whether I get approval or not. Sometimes I don't receive appreciation or approval and I am ok with it. Yes, it is nice to receive a thank-you, but I don't need it like I used to. My serving comes from being His beloved. He sees what I do. He tells me "thank you."

Another benefit of letting go of our idols is being able to have better relationships with others. As I see people as God's beloved and have realistic expectations, my relationships have become better. We will discuss healthy relationships in the next chapter.

Chapter Ten
Healthy Relationships

God created us to be in relationship with Him and with each other. Even though Adam had God and paradise all to himself, God saw that Adam needed another human being and created Eve. Our relationships can give us joy and add meaning to life. They help us grow to become all we were created to be. Our loved ones provide a place for our deep human needs: to be loved, heard, accepted, secure, respected and forgiven.

Unfortunately, anger, hurt, shame, trust issues, fear, control, codependency, idolatry, addictions--all affect our relationships. This is especially true for survivors. Those who have been abused often have trouble with trusting others as adults. We may even struggle with trusting ourselves.

My therapist told me I needed to trust my intuition. As I reflect back, I can see how this was true. I ignored "red flags" because I wanted certain relationships to work out. As a little girl, I needed the fun and attention that my friend's family gave me. Sometime around puberty, I suddenly stopped going there. I knew that what was happening with her father's behavior towards me was wrong but didn't know how to stop it. Both Mrs. Berger and my best friend kept saying "Why aren't you coming over anymore? What's going on with you? We miss you." This manipulation and blame made me feel guilty, as though I was the one to blame. I felt helpless for Lindsey, but I couldn't rescue her. I would blame myself when it for things I didn't cause or blame others when my needs were not met. Once I started therapy and entered into the process of spiritual formation, God gently peeled my blind spots away and showed me the places I needed to take ownership for my adult behaviors and change.

My psychologist told me, "You can't change people, you can only change yourself."

I show up and God does the work. Words cannot express how grateful I am. I have healthier boundaries now. I have some really good, life-giving relationships, especially with my immediate family and close friends. I try to give people the dignity to experience their own choices. I try to pray for God's best in others whether I am in their life or not. I don't take things personally like I used to. I still struggle with conflict but am willing to try and face it as it is inevitable. I am able to be in this place of the Beloved, having my love flow from there more often than before. I would like to share with you what has helped me come to this place.

Several books and spiritual practices helped to develop healthier relationships. Most were workbooks and shared in a small covenant group. Community is so important for growth as we learn from one another. Often, we can have blinders on to our weaknesses and even our strengths. We need encouragement as well as truth from one another to "change ourselves." You can decide if you are drawn to any of these workbooks.

Jesus is a great example in understanding friendship circles. He knew many people and ministered to many (feeding the five thousand, sending out the 72). He had a closer circle of friends and family: Mary his mother, Mary Magdalene, Lazarus, Mary, and Martha, to name a few. He had his core group of people: the twelve disciples. In His inner circle, He was closest to Peter, James, and John. We can have many people in our outer circles but only a few in our most intimate inner circle. Even our inner circle cannot meet all our needs. Jesus modeled that God was the one He turned to fill those deepest places in His heart, mind and soul.

"Intellectually, I knew that no human friendship could fulfill the deepest longing in my heart. I knew that only God could give me what I desired."

Henri Nouwen, author of *The Inner Voice of Love*[26]

I so agree with Henri. I hear women say, "I just don't feel God and I need a real person to love me." We were created for relationship with others. Yet I have learned in those dark, lonely places, no one can really fill me. Many times I hear women say, "No one is really there for me." People are limited. People are unique with different personalities, needs, and desires. People are flawed. People are "works in progress." People are God's beloved children. And I am a "people", too.

Only God can truly be there for us 24/7. You may not always feel His presence or His love and that is ok. I can't explain it but over time you will.

Giving the reality that we are all limited, I want to share some tools in this chapter how to have better relationships. Let's read my friend Nancy's story, who struggled with the pain of divorce.

You have heard the saying, "tall, dark and handsome?" Well, that is exactly who Ryan was. I might add, exciting, sanguine, and charming, who looked like Antonio Banderas. I met him at a dance. The other girls were all swooning over him as he walked toward us to where we were huddled together. He chose me to dance!

In the beginning our marriage was wonderful as we traveled together. Then we had two beautiful daughters. But just as happiness escalated, the bubble burst and trouble reared its ugly head. Ryan was using drugs. I would find signs and confront him. He would promise to quit but that never lasted. We were constantly fighting. He wasn't dependable. One time he just left me and my daughter at a concert. I was so upset.

Ryan would go to church with me. He would cry over the worship service and say he was remorseful. I felt some hope that He would find God and make a change in his life. There was a man at church who offered to mentor my husband, but he wasn't open to it. I also asked him to go to counseling with me. He went about three times and then quit. The counselor told me that if he did drugs around the kids, especially with them in the car and was caught, then the law could take my kids away. The light bulb inside me went on. I needed to get advice.

I had tried to hide Ryan's drug problem from my family, especially because my father was a detective in law enforcement. Yet I needed some advice, so I went to talk to my dad about the situation. He then informed me that Ryan had been arrested for soliciting sex from an undercover cop posing as a dancer in exchange for cocaine. I was in a state of shock. I knew I had to get out of my marriage.

I was a wreck. We separated. I moved in with my mother until I got my own apartment with my daughters. I would drop them off at school and then start crying, which lasted until I picked them up. I would stare at a tree outside my apartment, feeling numb and empty.

I went to church and asked the pastor to please pray that God would heal my marriage. Then I heard from Ryan, who begged for forgiveness, and said he would go to counseling. I thought this was my answer to prayer, so he moved back in. It didn't take long before we were back in the same place as before. I doubted God and remember one day praying out loud to Him, "I was having this wonderful time with you, God, and now I have all this chaos in my home again. Why? I thought you were answering my prayer? Why aren't you changing him? Am I not praying enough?" I had a hard time letting go. And I certainly didn't want the stigma: *Divorced.*

Then one day the phone rang. I picked it up, saying "hello?" and the person hung up. This happened again and then I picked up the phone saying who is this? This young woman on the phone answered shyly that she was my husband's daughter. What??!!

She was 17, his daughter and wanted to talk to him. Her age was in-between my daughters' ages at the time. I didn't want to accept it and I hung up the phone.

I confronted Ryan when he got home. He admitted it was true. He had an affair (actually several) while he was married to me and had another daughter. Hearing that just took my breath away. I felt shaky all over, not in reality, like I was in the movies. Once the initial shock subsided, I was so angry at him. How could you hide a child? Who is this person? How did I not see anything?? I can't even describe how upset I was. So I got the courage to ask him to leave and then filed for divorce.

It took time to get over it. It was a deep wound and it traumatized me. I lost confidence in myself and in my decisions. I had tremendous guilt about not protecting my daughters from his lies, his unfaithfulness and his drugs. I was depressed. I asked God, 'why?' I believed He was telling me that the enemy had his claws in Ryan. There were other people at church and the counselor who tried to help but he refused. God offered him love, forgiveness, restoration and help throughout the process, but again, Ryan refused. God does not impose himself on us. Like Al-Anon says, we can't change people. We can only change ourselves.

My wound was deep, and I started to fill it with work. There I got the affirmation I needed. I was very successful and this helped re-build my self-worth, which had been slowly decomposing in my marriage. I learned how to trust myself and my decisions again. I knew I could survive and provide for my daughters. I was becoming whole again. Sometimes, I struggle with getting my identity in my job and in busy-ness. Over time, I have learned some spiritual practices that help me remember that I am his beloved just as I am, whether I am working or not, busy or resting. Who I am today is not who I was in the past. Memorizing scripture verses has also helped me replace the lies with truth.

The main key in my healing process is forgiveness. It's a process. For the longest time, I wanted him to hurt like did. I didn't want anything more from him or anything to do with him. He never apologized to me. Yet, I came to a place where I didn't want anger or vengeance to control me any longer. I had to forgive Ryan for all the hurt he caused. We have learned to be cordial to one another and try to put the girls' needs first. I apologized to my daughters for my part in the whole situation and we have made amends. The hardest thing to do was forgive myself for my poor decisions. I don't want to blame the woman I used to be anymore. I have changed and become stronger. I have a Voice. I have loved ones and fellow believers who walked by my side, encouraging me and praying for me. I have a new husband who believes in me and encourages me to be the woman I was created to be. And I have my God who is with me always.

I am His beloved daughter, with whom He is well pleased.

Healthy Relationships

As I mentioned before, I struggled for years with facing conflict in my relationships. I would usually try to avoid it altogether. Part of this reason was because of me taking things personally, my faulty belief that anger was bad, and not having good boundaries. Another reason was that I had trouble choosing safe people. During my healing time or dark night of my soul (after my 50th birthday), I spent some time reflecting on my relationships. I pondered what being a safe person looked like. I reflected on who were safe people for me and who were not. I also learned how to have good boundaries. Today, I am able to respect others' boundaries as well have my own healthy boundaries. Although conflict can still be a challenge for me, I don't take it so personally and am able to deal with it in a healthier way. I cherish the safe people I have in my life today and try to be safe for them as well. Some insightful books and teachings for me came from Drs. Cloud and Townsend, actor Tyler Perry, Pat Springle and my first spiritual director, Caralie Norman.[27]

First, I will talk about what I learned from Caralie. She taught me how to "hold" differences. Often conflict arises with those who have different beliefs and opinions. Mature people do not get so defensive or critical when people differ strongly with them. The more secure and grounded I am, the more I don't take it personally or get my feelings hurt when conflict arises. Someone once said to me, "The thing about opinions is that everyone has one." I have seen people who don't even know each other scream obscenities over different political opinions! I can't control how people respond to me but I can choose how I respond to others, especially those who are different from me. I was encouraged to see these people as God's beloved, as works in progress, just as I am.

I also gained insight from books by Drs. Henry Cloud and John Townsend: *Boundaries*[28] and *Safe People.*[29] Having healthy boundaries tells us we are separate from one another. Knowing my boundaries helps protect me from unsafe people. Cloud and Townsend state that unsafe people are controllers, critics, irresponsible, and abandoners. Safe people are those who want to "dwell" with you, offer grace and speak the truth in love. I highly recommend their books and curriculum if your boundaries are weak or if you need to be aware of who is safe and who is not safe. The book also taught me how to be more of a safe person in my relationships.

As I mentioned in Chapter Seven, Pat Springle: *Untangling Relationships: A Christian Perspective on Codependency* [30]was life changing for me. I can feel compassion and come alongside others in pain, however I cannot take responsibility for their feelings or their journey. God and the person are the authors of their story. At times, I wanted to "fix" people so they wouldn't suffer the pain I felt. I also didn't want to trigger my own pain. Instead of seeing pain as good or bad, right or wrong, see it as a part of life, something that draws the person closer to God, allowing transformation if the person chooses. This new belief has led me to accept and feel my own pain and sit with others in theirs.

Finally I want to mention actor-playwright Tyler Perry.[31] He writes, in *Madea Goes to Jail*, "Life is like a tree. There are many leaves, they come and go and are there for a season. Mostly they take from the tree. Don't get mad at them because that is who they are. The branches are with you for a longer period of time. Be careful because as you change, grow and step out, they may fall off. The roots give life to the tree. They sustain the tree. You can only have 2 or 3 of those. Be grateful if you have some roots."

What Perry said gave me insight to my tree of life. Some relationships were in my life for only a season. Sadly, part of the breakups were because I did not handle conflict well. Also, as I have grown, I desire to be with people who are also growing, transforming on this deeper journey. Some people prefer the old me-- codependent and easy to push around. Others do not understand, nor do they want to hear about my healing journey with God. As Perry wrote, don't beat them up because that is where they are at. He also insists that if someone does not want to be with you then *let them go*.

From my research, reading, and my own experiences before setting healthy boundaries, I have learned that if we watch for the warning signs of unhealthy relationships, we can make sure our boundaries are strong. Things to heed include: always feeling on guard and that you must live up to someone else's standards; feeling irritated or not content when with them; feeling controlled, guilty, drained or abused; putting their goals and happiness above your own, or not allowing God to be in charge of the relationship. There are other signs as well. If you feel uneasy, unhappy, or unable to be yourself, be careful. On the other hand, here is what I learned and now desire in a healthy relationship:

- Encourage each other to grow closer to God.
- Encourage each other to grow emotionally.
- Want God's and life's best for each other.
- Acceptance or offer grace where we are at in life.
- Life-giving: we both feel energized, not drained nor empty.
- Give and take. Both listen to each other and share thoughts and feelings.
- Handle conflict by speaking truth in love, with the right motive.
- Celebrate the joyous times and offer silent compassion during suffering.
- Authentic, with realistic expectations of each other.
- Respect each other's boundaries.
- Treat him/her as I want him/her to treat me.
- Not needy, controlling, critical, demanding, irresponsible or jealous.

Reflection:

As you reflect on this list, what resonates with you?

_____

_____

Who is safe for you? Who is not? _____

_____

_____

With whom do you need to practice better boundaries? What does that look like? _____

_____

_____

As you reflect on this list, what are some growth areas for you to become a healthier spouse, friend, mother, etc.?

_____

_____

_____

Write your own list of what you desire in a close relationship.

_____

_____

_____

_____

Reflect on your list. Who has some of these qualities? Reflect on someone in your life who does not. What is God asking of you in these relationships?

_____

_____

_____

If you choose, draw your tree. Who are the leaves in your life? Who are the branches? The roots? What fruit (of the spirit) is on your tree? Which needs more watering?

What or who needs to be pruned from your tree (life)?

The Hardware Store

Amber: *One of the best tools I learned at Al-Anon was:* **"Don't go into the hardware store expecting to buy bread."**

This tool has been life changing for me in my relationships. If I desire nourishment from bread (e.g. encouragement), I cannot expect that from a hardware store. I can buy a hammer which is very good and useful for building structures and hanging pictures. However, a hammer does not provide the emotional support I need. If I want bread, or encouragement, I can to go to the bakery. In other words, I seek to get the encouragement I need from someone else or someplace else that can offer it. And here is the key: not to beat myself up because I didn't get bread or encouragement from that hardware store, and not to beat up the hardware store--for that is who he or she is, and that is what they are able to offer. I tell myself that I am okay the way, and the hardware store (i.e. a person in my life) is okay. We can't expect another human being to fulfill all our needs. I have learned over time to surrender my unrealistic expectations to God. Most of all, I get the encouragement and love I desire from God because His love is the only love that truly satisfies.

In your journal answer the following questions:

- Name someone you want a better relationship with.
- What do you want from them? Be honest and don't judge your desires.
- Are your expectations realistic or unrealistic?
- What need is this person able to meet? Maybe the hardware store can't give you encouragement but he or she can give you tools.
- What are your deeper needs in this relationship? (security, significance, respect, to be loved, heard, or valued, etc.)
- How are you able to meet their desires or needs?
- How do you feel when you can't meet someone's expectations of you?
- Are you able to talk to this person about your needs and expectations?

When you are ready, sit with God in silence.

- Breathe in and out slowly.
- Offer yourself compassion for not receiving what you need. Then offer the other person compassion for not being able to give that to you.
- Breathe in: *I am your Beloved,* breathe out: *he or she is Your beloved.* Breathe in: *I am okay,* breathe out: *he or she is okay.* Repeat this until you feel peace inside.
- Slowly let go and release your expectations to God.

Love Others as You Love Yourself . . . Love Your Enemies

Jesus tells us to love our enemies. He said it's easy to love those who love you; even the heathens do that. Yet loving those who don't love us is another story. Enemy is such a strong word. As I read in the psalms, David had many strong enemies who were out to kill him. Most of us don't experience enemies like David did, however we all experience "D.O.s."

A D.O. is a Different Other, Dislikable Other, Dysfunctional Other, Disagreeable Other, Draining Other, Drama Other or Detestable Other.

When we think of love, we think of the warm fuzzy feeling we have for those who are close to us. Jesus used the term "agape" (God-like love) and talked about treating others as you want to be treated. We don't have "phileo" (love for family and close friends) for everyone. We are asked to treat our D.O.s as we want to be treated.

Here are some practical suggestions:

If your D.O. is dysfunctional or draining for most people, then the best thing to do is show kindness with boundaries. Try to see them as God's beloved child, too.

If you are allowing yourself to be drained by them (some say, "suck the life out of me"), explore why you are doing that? Being co-dependent is not helpful for the person and not for you either. Perhaps you have a Messiah Complex (I can fix them, save them, help them).

I encourage you to know your call from God and guard it. Remember Jesus served in many ways: healing, casting out demons, feeding the hungry, teaching, helping the poor, etc. We each have certain gifting or calling. If I spend too much time with a Draining Other, then I won't have the energy or time to pour into those I am called to serve.

- What is your calling?
- How can you say "no" to someone or something so you can say "yes" to God's calling for you?

Pastor Mike Quinn once asked us, "Is there someone in your life who rubs you the wrong way, but doesn't rub others the wrong way?" This could be a Different Other or Disagreeable Other or Dislikable Other.

I try to explore what is going on inside of me that makes them rub me the wrong way, but not others. Psychologists say that sometimes we don't like someone because they remind us of something we don't like about ourselves. Or perhaps someone reminds us of someone who hurt us. On the next page is an exercise you can explore with God.

Reflection

Write the names of your D.O.s _____

_____

_____

What is it about them that bugs you?

_____

_____

_____

Why is this person difficult for you? Do they remind you of someone else or a trait in yourself that you do not like?

_____

_____

_____

What do I truly desire from this person? _____

_____

_____

Are there any unrealistic expectations that you have of them? They have of you? Or you have of yourself? _____

_____

_____

Is there a deeper need you have when you are with them? To be loved, valued, respected, heard, understood? _____

_____

_____

Do you need to forgive them? _____

_____

_____

How can you stay present, as His beloved, when you are with them? (Al-Anon calls this *Detach with love*). _____

_____

_____

Practical Suggestions for dealing with D.O.s:

You have a Helper, the Holy Spirit. Ask Him to help you.

If you know you are going to be with one, pray up.

If you are caught off guard, don't feel you have to say or do something if you are not ready.

Practice boundaries with love, especially with EGRs (Extra Grace Required), addicts and those with mental illness.

Try to put yourself in their shoes.

Try to listen to their story. This develops compassion.

Be compassionate in the moment, then move on if need to.

Detach with love.

See them as His beloved, too. They are children of God, just as you are.

Try to respectfully hold differences of opinions and beliefs, race, status, economics, religion etc.

Remember we are all works in progress. **Don't beat yourself up.**

Treat others as you want to be treated. Show kindness without being harsh or judgmental.

Rick Warren, pastor and author of *The Purpose-Driven Life,* and many other books, has said that feelings are not right or wrong, they are just feelings.[32] It's what we do with them that matters. We all need to be loved, valued, understood, and respected. Yet when we insist we NEED these things from certain people who cannot give them to us, we tend to criticize them or ourselves in our hearts. When I explore what is going on inside of me, then God can help me. This deeper healing brings about genuine peace, contentment and freedom. Exploring inside ourselves (examine my heart, O God) allows true transformation from God. Many people had unrealistic expectations of Jesus, but He knew who He was. And He moved on.

"Do not judge, or you too will be judged. For in the same way you judge others, you will be judged, and with the measure you use, it will be measured to you. Why do you look at the speck of sawdust in your brother's eye and pay no attention to the plank in your own eye? How can you say to your brother or sister, 'Let me take the speck out of your eye,' when all the time there is a plank in your own eye? You hypocrite, first take the plank out of your own eye, and then you will see clearly to remove the speck from your brother's eye."

Matthew 7:1-5 (NIV)

"Don't pick on people, jump on their failures, criticize their faults unless of course you want the same treatment. That critical spirit has a way of boomeranging. It's easy to see a smudge on your neighbor's face and be oblivious to the ugly sneer on your own. Do you have the nerve to say, 'Let me wash your face for you,' when own face is distorted by contempt? It's this whole traveling roadshow mentality all over again, playing a holier-than-thou part instead of just living your part. Wipe that ugly sneer off your own face, and you might be fit to offer a washcloth to your neighbor."

Matthew 7: 1-5 (MSG)

Richard Rohr, author of *Falling Upward* and founder of the Center for Action and Contemplation, [33] stated at a conference, "Jesus was a great psychologist" and quoted the passage above. I agree with him and yet this is a challenge. I also hear this passage distorted among Christians who accuse others of judging someone when maybe they are just disagreeing with the person. I have been guilty of this as well. I have learned to explore my own motive when I say something critical in my heart about someone else. Here are some questions to ask:

- When I judge, what is my tone? Is it condemning or am I discerning?

For example, a person who is critical is not safe for me to have in my inner circle. If my tone is condemning: beating them up for being critical, then this becomes judgmental. If on the other hand, my tone is discerning, putting up a boundary with love, then this is being wise.

I have been accused of being "judgey" when my motive was to speak truth. I lovingly tried to tell a friend that she dominated the conversations during small group. She wasn't ready to hear it and sadly our relationship ended. I can't be responsible for how another person will respond. I can only pray and be sure my motive is a genuine concern for them.

Another example is the difference between beliefs and opinions. We all have them and some of us can come across very strong. This may be misinterpreted as being judgmental. Maybe the person isn't being critical; they just need to be right or be heard.

- Explore the differences between beliefs, opinions and convictions. As I mentioned earlier, I learned this from Caralie Norman. For example, an opinion could be a preference for a certain kind of worship music in church. I have seen people argue over this. A belief could be a certain theology. There have been many arguments over whether or not women should be pastors/priests in a church, for another example. A conviction is something we rarely argue about because it is so true such as murder is wrong. We all have are opinions, beliefs, and convictions. Spend some time knowing what yours are. Be willing to listen. Ask yourself if this is worth arguing over. Try to agree to disagree.
- If your tone is condemning or critical, explore why? Look at your deep desires and needs again. Is something not being met?

For example, I was listening to a woman who was saying she didn't like her "judgey" spirit, especially when she was with one particular friend. As we spent time exploring, she realized she struggled with envy. This friend had life financially easy and didn't have to worry about retirement like she did.

- Take some time to explore. Look at someone in your life you feel judged or criticized by.
- What is going on in their life? Try to put yourself in their shoes. This doesn't make it right, just helps us to understand.
- Is this difference in opinions, beliefs, and convictions? Can you try to see things from their perspective?
- Is this a critical person with whom you need to establish boundaries? How?
- Now take some time and see who you are "judgey" towards. What are you saying in your head/heart?
- Is there a deeper need or desire that is not being met by them? By life? By God?
- What is your "plank" that you need to work on? Often, we criticize things in others that we don't like about ourselves.
- Do you need to enter into changing and surrendering expectations? (See hardware exercise.)
- Do you need to enter into forgiveness? This is presented in Chapter 12.

Love

> Love never gives up
>
> Love cares more for others than for self
>
> Love doesn't want what it doesn't have
>
> Love doesn't strut
>
> Love doesn't have a swelled head
>
> Love doesn't force itself on others
>
> Love isn't always "me first"
>
> Love doesn't fly off the handle
>
> Love doesn't keep score of the sins of others
>
> Love doesn't revel when others grovel
>
> Love doesn't take pleasure in the flowering of truth
>
> Love is patient, Love is kind (NIV)
>
> Love trusts God always
>
> Love never looks back
>
> Love keeps going to the end
>
> 1 Corinthians 13 (MSG)

As you reflect on this list, what areas of loving do you do well? _____
_____

What areas do you need to do better? _____
_____

Who provides love for you and in what way? _____
_____

How can you become more loving in your relationships? _____
_____

I was taking a class long ago in psychology and the professor asked us this question:

Do you love others because of who they are or do you love others because of the way they make you feel about yourself?

Wow! I don't know anyone who truly loves like that. Usually, I love people who make me feel good about myself. I am so grateful our God loves us for who we are.

Relationships have been the joy of life for me and also deep sorrow. Some people have not lived up to my expectations. And I know I have not lived up to certain people's expectations. I do have much healthier boundaries and I do pray for God's best for people even if I don't feel valued by them. Spending time with God, surrendering my expectations and allowing Him to fill my soul has been life changing for me. Jesus has become my best friend. He loves me, He listens to me, He delights in me.

We are a D.O. – Delightful Other to God!

In summary, practice these principles to receive more satisfaction in relationships:

- Choose safe people.
- Be a safe person.
- Have good boundaries.
- Do not judge.
- Love others as you love yourself. Treat others as you want to be treated.
- Have realistic expectations and surrender unrealistic expectations to God.
- Be grateful for the good things/gifts that the relationship brings.
- See this person as a child of God . . . a work in progress . . . the Beloved as you are.
- Pray for God's best for all your relationships.

Relationships bring love and hate, joy and hurt, fun and disappointment. We desire the positive but not the negative. Although we cannot change people, God can change us. If we truly want to experience freedom and more of the abundant life, then the key is forgiveness and letting go. Sometimes we need to grieve what was lost before we can let go. Let's look at grief in the next chapter.

Chapter Eleven
Grief

Grief is a part of our healing process. Sadly, it is not valued in our culture. We are told to move on too quickly, or are given one of many Christian platitudes such as: "This is God's will." People in mourning are often avoided or brushed aside.

Sometimes it is hard to heal, to forgive and let go if we haven't grieved over what was lost. Usually when people think of grief, they think of the loss of loved ones. I give myself permission to grieve all my losses with God. I did grieve over the loss of my parents who were dear to me. I also grieved over the wounds of my childhood. I mourned over my mistakes. I still am sad over several broken relationships because of my own brokenness. Like women whom I have journeyed with, we had to grieve over the loss of being sexualized before we were ready, having something precious taken from us without permission. We all have felt sorrow over broken relationships, past poor choices, unanswered prayers and dreams that never came true.

I have learned much about grief from journeying with those who have experienced trauma and who have lost loved ones. I want to share some of their stories with you along with two women, both named Mary, in Scripture who were precious to Jesus and who mourned deeply over His death.

Missy: *When I saw the three-month old fetus in the jar, my peripheral vision started to dim. I felt an overwhelming sense of remorse and grief over the loss of this baby and the one I aborted. After this experience is when my grieving process started.*

Jane: *Why did God allow this to happen? I still struggle to this day. Grief comes and goes. Being angry at God and lamenting to him, as David did in the Psalms, has been helping me heal.*

The crowds were gathered. The shouting and screaming was overwhelming. I tried desperately to make my way through the city gates. What is going on? Where is my son? I heard people saying "arrested," "guilty," "crucifixion…" what?? I could not believe this. This isn't the way it was supposed to be. I pushed my way desperately through the streets.

Then I saw him. My son, carrying a cross. He was bleeding all over his body. His face was black and blue. Someone had put this crown of thorns on his head. I opened my mouth to cry out: "Get that off of him! Stop whipping him! Leave him alone!" Yet nothing was able to come out.

Then he saw me. The tears welled up in both our eyes. I ran to him and tried to touch him but the soldiers would not let me. "Why?" I cried, 'Why?" Then our eyes locked. We held each other in our hearts in that brief moment.

I witnessed the whole horrible event. They stripped him of his clothes and then nailed my son to the cross. I wept profoundly as I stood there, helpless, just watching him die. I couldn't believe that he was thinking of me as he was dying, asking John to take care of me. So like my son, always thinking of others, always forgiving others and always loving others. In the midst of my tears, I am proud of my son, for all he did and for all he gave.

When he gave up his spirit, I felt like I died as well. Words cannot express the grief and loss I felt. The sky turned dark and lightning struck. One of the soldiers said, "Surely this must be the son of God." In the midst of my pain, I held on to this in my grieving heart.

After a few hours, they took him down and placed him in my arms. "My son, my son," I cried through my tears. "I remember when you were little and you played among the cobbled stone roads in Nazareth. You learned from Joseph how to do carpentry and created such beauty. You started a ministry to help the poor, feed the hungry, heal the sick, cast out demons. And now you have given the most precious gift of all, your life. I am so proud of the man you were. I love you more than you know. I will think of you all my days."

I miss you terribly. I will always treasure you in my heart.

My son Dave was very loving, gracious, talented and energetic. He was very close to me. Yet he had a serious mental health issue. Depression emerged when he was in high school and started experimenting with drugs.

As a young adult, he still had bouts of depression but seemed to be functioning well and was a teacher. Dave and his wife were married for a year when he found out she didn't really love him and was having an affair. They divorced. This was a shock to me and devastating for my son. He entered into a dark depression, starting using methamphetamine by injection.

This was so difficult for me to believe. I started to volunteer in his classroom so I could help him out. I could see he wasn't with it. I thought he was just depressed and would pull through it. I started paying the bills for him. I had no idea he was using the money for drugs. I was unaware at that time that I was codependent, an enabler.

One day, he didn't show up for work. He had gone to the railroad tracks and was going to jump in the front of the train and end his life. He declared that his life wasn't worth living. I felt helpless as I saw my beloved son so full of shame and despair. I was disappointed that I didn't see the signs before. I decided to seek out therapy and Al-Anon. My son went into a residential program, got the help he needed, got sober and became active in AA. This is where he met his second wife.

They had their first son together. He brought so much joy to my son. But it didn't take long for Dave to sink back into that pit of despair. He suffered from migraines as a result of a car accident. He also had chronic back pain which was even worse after back surgery. He was on multiple medications for pain and for depression. He overdosed on his prescription medications and was hospitalized on several occasions.

Then one Saturday, he came over to our house. He was in so much inner turmoil, he broke down and cried. I just listened with compassionate love while feeling helpless at the same time. Al-Anon had taught me the three C's. I didn't cause it. I can't control it. I can't cure it. All I could do was offer compassion and love, while surrendering my son and his turmoil to God.

The next day, he called me and asked if I could drive him to go get a pain shot. I was torn because I was in my class and Al-Anon encouraged me to take care of myself and not be an enabler to my son. I apologized and said I couldn't do it this time and asked him if he could find his own way of getting there. He said, "That is fine, Mom. Don't worry about it."

That was the last time I talked to him.

Dave had left his house that night after a heated argument with his wife. He took a gun with him. The police and a few neighbors began searching for him. I waited behind in the house with my grandson.

I just sat there filled with worry and anxiety. I wondered if my son was cold? What was he thinking? Where was he? What was he doing? My heart was just racing. I remembered the prayer of Detachment that I learned in Al-Anon. If a crisis is going to happen, it is going to happen. I cannot control or change the situation. I could not "will" my son to survive. He was getting all the help he could at the time. I prayed the Serenity Prayer over and over in my heart:

God, grant me the serenity to accept the things I cannot change, the courage to change the things I can, and the wisdom to know the difference.

Then at 7 am, the police showed up at the door. I just looked into their faces and I knew. "Is he gone?" I asked. They replied, "Yes, he is."

My son, my beloved son, was lying across the street, in the neighbor's yard in a pool of blood. He had shot himself in the head. I fell into shock. I couldn't cry. I couldn't feel. I just stuffed everything.

He took his life 3 days before his 38th birthday. I read him a birthday card at his funeral. I told him that I remember when he first skinned his knees. This would be the easiest wound he would have to deal with. I wish I could shield him from life's wounds but I could not. I raised him the best I could. I told him how proud I was of the man he was: a good man, a kind man. And that I would miss him terribly.

How do I come out of a tragedy like this? Grief is a process. It's like going up and down over hills and valleys. Each time I go down a little less deeply in the valley than the day before. I don't want this to be the identifier of my life. I have done a lot of lamenting. Through a spiritual direction group, I learned that David lamented throughout the psalms as well as sang praises to God. He was considered a man after God's heart. If David lamented, then so could I. I know it's ok to be angry at God for what happened. He is a big God and can take it. He wants to hear my whole heart, both when praising and when angry.

I had to fight and wrestle with the question, "How could God do this? How could a good God allow this to happen?" I believe that God grieved over what happened. He does allow things to happen to us and I may not know why. I do know He can help me through it. What is important is how I react to what has happened over time. Healing is a process.

What was so hard for me was Dave dying by his own hand. How did I fail my son? I know that I did not cause this, intellectually. Yet at times, I struggle with failure as a mother. Getting some insight on Borderline Personality Disorder has helped me understand there really was a difference in my son's brain. He suffered terribly from mental illness. He may have felt that there was no other way. As reflect, I know I did the best I could as a mother, to the best of my ability.

I also struggled because I grew up hearing in church that if one commits suicide, then they go to hell. I needed to see what the Bible said about suicide. It's mentioned in the Bible seven times, and it does not say people who take their own lives go to hell. Only the sin of rejecting God or blaspheming the Holy Spirit is unforgivable. Dave did not reject God. He was full of shame, mental illness, and prescription drugs. God can forgive this and He has forgiven Dave.

I miss him terribly. I will always treasure him in my heart.

Penitent Magdalene (1453-1455) by Donatello (1475-1564)
Museo dell'Opera del Duomo, Florence, Italy

Where do I begin? There is so much to tell. My soul was tormented day and night by demonic spirits. The lies: "I am not good enough, I am not worthy, I have nothing to offer," played over and over in my head. These accusations of not being valued and significant left me feeling hopeless, destitute and so alone.

Then He walked into my life. He saw my torment and felt such compassion towards me. With such power and authority, He commanded the demons to leave my body and my soul. I twisted and screamed out as each one departed until my limp, lifeless body fell to the floor. Then He told me to rise. As I slowly did, a feeling came over me that I have never felt before. I felt loved, worthy, valued, gifted with a purpose. I felt so accepted by this man, Jesus. My gratitude was beyond words...deeper than I could ever express. All I knew was that I was free!

From then on, I followed him. He gathered twelve men to become his closest disciples. Many others followed him along the way. Some fell away because Jesus wasn't the conquer-the-Romans King they wanted him to be. He spoke of a different kingdom, one not of this world but of heaven, a place with no more suffering, no more tears. I didn't fully understand, yet I knew I wanted to follow him more than anything. I saw him perform many miracles. He healed the sick, the deaf, the blind and the lepers. He cast out demons, fed the five thousand, and so much more. He taught in the synagogues, along the lakeshore and in people's houses with power and authority. He poured himself into his closest followers with teaching, encouraging them with loving truth. I also witnessed how he took time out for himself, to pray in silence and solitude, to nap and rest, and to have fun. I felt so honored to be a part of his life here on earth.

I followed him until the end. I was there...with the women...with his mother and John. I felt so helpless. To see him suffering, broken, bleeding, hanging naked upon that cross. I couldn't do anything to help, fix or save him. Tears overflowed from my eyes as I was in a whirlwind of grief.

I arose early on Sunday, after Passover, to anoint his body. They laid him in the tomb quickly on Friday and everyone was getting ready for Passover, which started at sundown. I wanted to give him a proper Jewish anointing and burial. When I arrived at the tomb, I was caught off guard. The stone had been moved from the entrance to the tomb. Wondering what was happening; I hurried to the entrance and went inside. The tomb was empty! There were strips of linen but no body. Tears streamed from my face. Then I saw two angels, clothed in white, seated where my Lord's body was laid. They asked me, "Woman, why are you crying?" I answered them, "they have taken my Lord away and I don't know where they put him."

As I turned around, a man I didn't recognize was standing there. He spoke to me and asked why I was crying and who I was looking for? Thinking he was the gardener, I said, "Sir, if you have carried him away, tell me where you have put him and I will get him." Then he looked at me with eyes full of love and said my name, "Mary."

"RABONI!!!" I cried. It was Jesus! Standing in front of me. More radiant than before. Transformed . . . light . . . beautiful! I was ecstatic and threw myself at his feet and hugged him. He hugged me, too briefly, and then said, "Don't hold onto me for I have not yet returned to the Father. Go instead to my brothers and tell them I am returning to my Father and your Father, to my God and your God." I said, "Yes, Lord!" and ran to tell the others with the news:

"I have seen the Lord, I have seen Him!!!"

I love this statue of Mary Magdalene carved in wood by Donatello. I spent some time in the Duomo museum in Italy just gazing at her. Although it may be hard to tell in this photo, Donatello had a way of capturing her feelings in her face. I could almost hear her say: *you can't imagine my life over the last few years.* She really did experience healing from Jesus. And she had the honor of following Him although she is not called an apostle. She is often confused with other Marys in the Bible, namely the sinful woman who washes Jesus' feet with her hair and Mary of Bethany, sister of Lazarus. She was from the town of Magdala, on the Sea of Galilee. She had been inflicted with seven demons when she met Jesus. He cast them out and freed her from bondage. She was free from bondage and followed him ever since.

Unlike the disciples who fled in fear, except for John, Mary was present at the crucifixion. She was weeping and grieving with the other women. She could not fix Jesus or rescue Him. She could only offer her silent, compassionate presence. She was the first one He appeared to on that Sunday morning which we call Easter.

Her model is what I believe we need to offer when someone is grieving. She couldn't fix Jesus' pain on the cross. All she could offer was her presence. She offered silent compassion. I encourage you to "hold" the person who is grieving in silent compassion. I also encourage you to offer yourself this same silent compassion if you are grieving. Instead of "getting over it" too quickly or stuffing it inside, allow yourself time to grieve like Mary Magdalene did at the cross. For Mary, the joy did come when she finally realized Jesus was there but not without a period of grief. Until your joy returns or you create a new normal, allow yourself to sit in the sadness, the grief, and the disappointment. Do the same for another as you sit with them in their pain. God will bring healing in His time.

On the this page is a reflection and a prayer of silent compassion followed by a list on what is helpful and what is not helpful to say to someone who is grieving.

Reflection

As you gaze at the statue of Mary Magdalene, what do you notice?_____
_____
_____

Like Mary was initially in despair at the cross, where are you feeling like this?_____
_____
_____

How do you feel that He is here with you in your despair, your grief? _____
_____
_____

Like Mary at the tomb, how do you feel when He calls you by name?
_____
_____

How is God speaking to you through the story of Mary Magdalene? _____
_____
_____
_____

Prayer of Silent Compassion

- Imagine yourself as Mary at the cross. Close your eyes.
- Breathe in and breathe out compassion.
- Sit in silence and offer compassion to Jesus.
- After a few moments, offer compassion to the thief on the cross (whoever the thief is in your life).
- Offer compassion to Mary, Jesus' mother.
- Now offer silent compassion to someone else who is grieving.
- Now offer and receive compassion to yourself.

Helpful things to say to one who is grieving

- I am sorry for your loss.
- I can't imagine what you are feeling now.
- May I sit with you for a moment?
- I love you.
- I am here for you.
- I know your (son) loved you and you will miss him very much.

Not so helpful things to say

- They are in heaven.
- He/she is not suffering anymore.
- You will see them again in heaven.
- It's a blessing they are not in pain now.
- Well, you should be over that now.
- Well, that happened so long ago.
- Dead silence.
- Why did you allow that to happen?
- Look at the positive side.
- Don't cry.
- Get over it.
- It's time to move on.
- It's God's will.

What do you identify with on this list?

What could you add to this list?

Grief Prayer Practice:

Sit in quiet with God. Ask yourself: what did I miss out on? What or who have I lost? In your journal or on a piece of paper, write your list.

Examples:

Loss of relationship through death, conflict, or drifting apart

Loss of material possessions   Unanswered prayer

Loss of a dream   Loss of a trophy or prize

Loss of job or career path   Loss of health

Loss of a healthy childhood   Unmet desires

Loss of loving family members, relatives, clergy, teachers etc.

- Whatever it is, take some time and allow yourself to grieve.
- Allow the feelings (sadness, disappointment, hurt, regrets, etc.) to happen and just sit with them.
- Feel them. It is ok. Try not to end this time too quickly as sitting with our feelings is necessary in order to release it.
- Offer compassion to your life. Offer compassion to yourself.
- You may want to mourn with God (Chap. 3) or with Jesus in the garden (Chapter 5). Remember He is/was grieved by what happened to you.
- When you are ready, ask for His help and release it to God.
- Receive God's compassion for you. Allow Him to comfort you.

You may want to use the pictures of the Garden Tomb in Israel on the next page. Some believe that this is where Jesus was buried.

Jane: *Grief is a process. I still struggle with the loss of my son. I may never "get over it" but with God's help, I can get through it.*

Everyone grieves differently. Try not to compare your grief process to others.

Grief comes and goes. It is normal to feel joy one moment and then suddenly feel sadness the next.

The Garden Tomb in Jerusalem, photo by Ron Richardson

Woman weeping and praying inside the Garden Tomb where some believe Jesus was buried.

The Model of Jesus

Jesus grieved over Jerusalem. God longed to gather His children of Israel back to Him as a mother hen gathers her chicks (Luke 13:34-35).

Jesus told the women he met, as he carried the cross to His death, to not weep for Him but to weep for Jerusalem (Luke 23:28).

He grieved over loved ones who died. When He heard his cousin, John the Baptist, was beheaded, He got in a boat and retreated to a solitary place (Matthew 12:14-13:1a).

He wept over the loss of His dear friend, Lazarus, even though He knew he would be resurrected (John 11:35).

Jesus grieved for Himself in the garden. He sweat tears of blood and was overwhelmed with sorrow (Mark 14:32-36, Matthew 26:36-39, Luke 22:44).

A dear friend of mine lost a sibling in a horrible car accident. Then a short time later, he lost another sibling to illness. He told me the shortest verse in scripture helped him grieve: Jesus wept (John 11:35). It is ok to cry. Jesus did. He even wept tears of blood over himself. I believe God is grieved by what happened to me and in all my losses. He grieves over what happened to you and your losses. He understands.

Chapter Twelve
Forgiveness and Letting Go

"Let it go." "Forgive." "Move on." How many times have I heard this? Or more recently: "Get over it." It's not always easy and often takes time. **This is especially true for those who have been traumatized.** I have noticed in my life when I hold a grudge in my heart, joy, peace, love, and freedom are stifled. When I forgive and release the anger, hurt, shame and resentment caused by the wounds of life, I can live more freely as His beloved.

Clara: *I developed a bitter root judgment toward my mother and stepfather. I judged them for being poor parents, not safe, not trustworthy and a whole lot more. I had so much resentment, anger and bitterness towards my stepfather. Over time, with Healing Prayer, I was able to let go and forgive them.*

Amber: *I had a harder time forgiving my dad than the boy who molested me because my dad did nothing to protect me. It took a long time to let go and let God, a practice taught by Al-Anon, that I still use to this day.*

Pamela: *It took me a long time to forgive as my father did to me what no father should do. Through healing prayer and writing him a letter, I was able to let go. I can honestly say now that I look forward to seeing him in heaven as he will be fully transformed, and so will I.*

Missy: *I feel no shame for my past, for having the abortion. I know He forgave me. He doesn't hold anything against me and doesn't keep bringing my past up again. I also learned how to forgive myself as I am no longer that same woman.*

Nancy: *The key in my healing process is forgiveness. It is a process. For the longest time, I wanted him to hurt like I did. Even though he never apologized to me, I was able to let it go.*

Maddison: *Forgiving my mom and her boyfriend took a long time. It was hard to let go of the pain that both my mom and the therapist thought I made the whole thing up. Jesus has brought healing to me especially through serving the poor and the lost.*

Mariah: *It took a long time. I was able to forgive my mother on her death bed.*

Beth: *I felt God move through me as I forgave my mother. I can't explain it but I am free!*

One woman who had been sexually abused asked me, "Do I really need to forgive him?" "Yes," I answered, "because the bitter poison only kills you."

A centuries-old saying is that not forgiving someone is like drinking poison and waiting for the other person to die. The unknown original source of this well-known analogy recognized that it takes a huge amount of emotional and mental energy to hold tightly to resentment and pain. This can sicken or even kill us.

I have forgiven Mr. Berger. I am not 100% sure but I do believe he molested his own daughters. My psychologist said a high percentage of men who are perpetrators molest their own daughters. Reflecting back, I can see now that when Lindsey entered puberty, she exhibited behaviors of an abused child. I do know he molested some of the other little girls in the neighborhood as I witnessed it. I believe God was angry at him and grieved over what happened to me. I am not sure, but I think Mr. Berger was sexually abused as a child. This forgiveness process I went through does not in any way accept his behavior. I never received an apology. He is probably not alive. I chose to forgive anyway. And I live in peace.

I have also forgiven my dad for his raging anger. I remember the day I finally stood up to him. I was driving him to his doctor's appointment and he started yelling at me in the car. I couldn't take it anymore and let him know. I finally used my voice. "Stop!" I yelled back. "I am not going to take this anymore. If you keep yelling at me then find someone else to drive you." He suddenly got quiet. We drove the rest of the way in silence.

The next day, he blamed me for yelling at him, saying he had never seen me do this before and was concerned about me. I didn't take on the blame this time. Although it was really hard for me, I am proud of myself for using my voice. He never yelled at me again. I let go of my dad not owning his part. I knew he loved me in his own way. It saddens me he did not deal with his anger as his life could have been so much better. We did make peace before he died even though I didn't receive an apology. I was able to let go and now I live in freedom.

Try to be open to receive and offer forgiveness. You will be the one who benefits greatly. Holding on to the past only hurts you. I pray and hope you will choose forgiveness. I know it is really hard. I get it. Forgiveness is a process and it's ok to take small steps. It may help to explain what it is and what it is not which I do in this chapter. First I want to share a powerful story of forgiveness from Beth, a woman who was in one of my Not Alone groups.

Beth's Story

I was five years old. I shared a room with my sister but she was not there that night. My father came in wearing only his boxer shorts. He got in bed and started doing things to me with his penis. I was so startled and somehow I ran out of the house and to the police station. I stood in the station, terrified, in my pajamas. The police called my parents who came and picked me up. They were so nice and grateful to the police. But when we got home, I got a beating like you wouldn't believe.

From then on, I kept silent. I couldn't sleep because I was so afraid he would come in my room. I started falling asleep in school. The teacher called my parents. All I heard was how stupid I was and that I was good for nothing. My mom even told me I was ugly.

My life from five to 10 is a blur. I remember trying to protect my siblings but I couldn't. I was no match for my dad. I just wanted to be out of the house so I got a job at ten years old selling T.V guide books door to door (this was back in the day with no child labor laws). I opened a savings account and had saved a large sum of money saved by the time I was 18. Back then, I didn't need my parent's permission to open an account. I coped by being independent. Every day I looked at that T.V. guide and said I was going to be on T.V. someday. I had to prove I could do it and that I was not a good for nothing. I moved out of the house as soon as I could.

My parents were racist. I didn't understand how they could think white people were better than people of a different ethnic background. I didn't feel that way. Actually, I met this young Mexican man who was so gorgeous I felt he was Adonis! (a Greek god who was very handsome). My mother said that Mexicans will rape and kill people. I didn't listen to her. This young man asked me out one night to a bonfire. He asked me? Really? I was such a nerd. Of course I said yes. Soon after we dated, fell in love and got married.

My parents disowned me. They cut me out of their lives for marrying a Mexican. We had four sons together and they disowned them as well, along with my brother who was gay. I grieved over the loss of a healthy, loving extended family. I focused on raising my own family, desiring my own to be in loving environment not the dysfunctional and messy one I was raised in. Sadly, one day I found out many other women also saw my husband as a gorgeous Adonis and he was cheating on me. He was also abusive. I came to the realization that I had married someone like my dad. Divorce was inevitable. My home was a mess.

After our divorce, I got my life back together and decided to fulfill my dream of being on television. I remember selling those T.V. guide books as a little girl telling myself I was going to be on T.V. someday. I was going to prove that I was not ugly and stupid. I had a contract with ABC for 11 years appearing on the nightly news! Reflecting back now, I can see how my identity was in being successful.

I also coped by being a challenger. My parents did not believe in God when I was growing up. So I wanted to know who God was and if He existed or not. I discovered He did. I became a believer and joined the Catholic faith. With God, therapy and time, I found a new life and a new husband. I had a successful T.V. career. I really felt I was going was going to be ok.

Over the next few years, the commandment: *Honor Thy Father and Mother* started tugging at my heart. I had a hard time understanding what God meant. He didn't say I only had to honor them if they were good to me or its ok to disown them since they were nasty to me. I asked God what was going on inside me? What was He trying to tell me?

Then I got the phone call. And from a brother I never met. My mom was dying and wanted to see me. I hadn't seen her in 15 years. My father passed years before and I hadn't seen him either since I was disowned. But now I am faced with whether or not to go see my mother. She knew what my father was doing to us kids. And she did nothing. I asked my brother why he felt responsible for taking care of mother. He told me that our parents were in great pain to do what they did to all of us. Then he said he felt convicted by the commandment: *Honor thy mother and father.* I hung up the phone and started crying.

This phone call came during Lent and while I was in a *Not Alone* group. We talked about God's grace and unconditional love and how forgiveness was crucial to healing and genuine transformation. My group was so supportive. I wanted to honor her as God's daughter, not for what she did to me. I wanted to go and just show mercy and offer forgiveness.

When I arrived at my mother's home, I was nervous, cautious and quite reserved. She put her arms around me. My heart was like an icicle. I could feel it slowly melting. I kept praying, pleading with God to help me forgive my mom. I felt remorse that I did not have loving feelings towards her. We talked for awhile. Or should I say she talked for awhile. Never asked me about me or my boys. I just sat there being polite.

All of a sudden, she looked me straight in the eyes and said, *"I would back my man no matter what he did."*

Then it happened. Something I can't explain…a true miracle! I felt God's power and extravagant love wash over me. I was so filled that I was able to show love and mercy towards my mother even though she didn't apologize. I finally understood what God's unconditional love, grace and mercy was all about.

My relationship with God has changed tremendously. I had to forgive those who hurt me the most. The shackles that had kept me in bondage all these years were finally released. I can't explain it…*I am free.*

Forgiveness

People get confused about forgiveness and letting go. I have heard some say, "He/she doesn't deserve forgiveness," or "That lets them off the hook," or "Then it's all my fault." The following explanation of forgiveness was presented by Sheryl Fleisher [34] which I have adapted. It is important to understand what forgiveness is and what it is not.

Forgiveness is not forgetting. It is healthy for us to recognize hurtful behavior, such as emotional or physical abuse, so we can have appropriate boundaries.

Forgiveness does not always lead to reconciliation. Trust may be broken. This person may not be safe. We can choose with whom we spend our time. Scripture tells that Paul and Barnabas served together, had a disagreement, split up and each went their own way. Both men were God's beloved and both chosen to serve Him, just not together.

Forgiveness is not condoning the other person's behavior. We think they will get away with it if we forgive. Or we think that makes them right and we are wrong. Not true. God tells us that vengeance is His. He is the judge and He will settle everything. We are to let go and let God.

Forgiveness means seeking justice. We can forgive and still hold people accountable for consequences. If someone commits a felony, justice can be served in court. Forgiveness is a process and needs to follow so the wound can heal.

Forgiveness is a process. Jesus told his disciples to forgive 77 times (Matt. 18:21-22). In other words, more than once. Each time we confess, Jesus forgives us. There are people in our lives who hurt us more than once. Just seeing someone again who hurt you in the past might stir up those old feelings. It doesn't mean you haven't forgiven as it's not about forgetting. It's about giving this person and hurt over to God again so we can move on.

Forgiveness is no longer seeking revenge or accusing them in your heart or to others. God tells us that vengeance is His. He will take care of it. He wants us to stop the "accusing video" from playing again and again because it only hurts us. If I spend my time rehearsing the video, it draws me away from God, instead of filling my thoughts with whatever is pleasing to Him. If we are consumed with revenge, bitterness can seep in like a cancer to our soul. This will keep us "stuck in the muck" so it will be difficult to serve God and others from a place of love.

Forgiveness is for our sake! We can be free in our hearts. Free to serve. Free to love. Free to celebrate being His Beloved. Free to experience more love, faith, hope, joy, peace, and kindness. We need forgiveness for our sins and to extend forgiveness to others. (John 20:20) *We know we have forgiven, when we no longer play the video. We stop accusing them in our hearts. We stop creating dissension or bad mouthing them to others.* Bitterness transforms into internal peace.

Missy's Story

I was raised in a home with parents who went through the depression era. That experience took its toll on their parenting. They were both stuck emotionally at a young age. My father was a rage-aholic. It was his way or the highway. He would bully us kids. My mother was not in touch with her femininity and she developed a crusty exterior to survive her childhood. No softness, no tears, no apologies were allowed in my home. The only emotion shown was anger.

I felt like a burden. My needs and wants didn't matter. I was not taught about decisions and consequences. I am not blaming my parents. I was just affected by the upbringing in my home.

When I finally moved out and went to college, I went crazy and rebelled. I became pregnant. The guy left me. I remember saying to myself that I would rather die than tell my parents so I decided to have an abortion. This happened in the 60's when abortion was illegal. I found someone who did abortions. I was three months pregnant. One day, this guy named Spike told me where to be on a corner, at night in downtown Chicago. I went and waited on the corner. A black car with smoked windows pulled up and told me to get in. I remember sitting in this apartment building in a room with some other girls. When it was my turn, I went into the room with the doctor and his nurse and got on the table….no anesthesia….and then it was done. I went home and went on with my life.

The 70's came along and I got married. George and I got into the "open marriage" scene with wife swapping, Jacuzzi orgy parties, swinging. I slept with so many men, I can't count them all. Sex did not mean intimacy to me, it was just a sport, just having fun.

We ended up divorced. For the next 10 years of my life, I was sleeping with every Tom, Dick and Harry. I got into New Age, crystals, EST, and self-improvement.

Then I met Mark. He was so different than the other men I knew. He was a strong Christian and led me to the Lord. We eventually married.

After my conversion, I remember feeling such relief, that I didn't need to do life by myself anymore. I was grateful how Christ saved me from some situations that could have been so much worse. I was forgiven for my promiscuity. Yet I hadn't dealt with the abortion.

One day we decided to go to the Science Museum. Somehow Mark and I got separated and I was alone. As I entered a room, I saw babies in jars of formaldehyde at different stages of life. There I saw a three-month old baby. All of sudden, my peripheral vision started to darken and I almost passed out. I felt so much remorse as this was a similar age as the fetus I aborted, that I murdered.

After this encounter, my grieving started. I felt so much remorse and asked for forgiveness. I have a sense my baby was a girl. And I wonder what her life would have been like. Although I felt tremendous grief, I did not feel guilt or shame because I was forgiven. I was able to forgive myself because that young girl, who was very different from me now, made a choice. I was a new woman in Christ and experienced His grace and He wiped my slate clean.

I don't feel shame about my promiscuity as I am forgiven. I am so grateful. It could have been so much worse; I could have died on that table during the frightful night in Chicago. However, I do admit there are consequences for my behavior. I still don't trust men. I get more emotional gratification from women. And I have difficulty with being vulnerable in my relationships. I don't like to call sex "making love" because I learned love and sex are separate. I don't see sex as the same as intimacy. I still have issues in this area and will need to deal with it the rest of my life. True, I am forgiven and I know God loves me. The shame and guilt are gone. I am not in bondage to my past even though there are consequences to the choices I made.

So I decided to make a difference. I became a Marriage and Family Therapist. I have a tremendous passion for children and troubled teens. I have helped many women accept forgiveness and forgive themselves. I encourage them to know that who they are in Christ is not based on their past behavior.

We truly are forgiven and free to live as beloved daughters of God.

Supper in the House of Simon the Pharisee by Moretto da Brescia (1550-54)

Now one of the Pharisees invited Jesus to have dinner with him, so he went to the Pharisee's house and reclined at the table. When a woman who had lived a sinful life in that town learned that Jesus was eating at the Pharisee's house, she brought an alabaster jar of perfume. And as she stood behind him at his fee weeping, she began to wet his feet with her tears. Then she wiped them with her hair, kissed them and poured perfume on them.

When the Pharisee who had invited him saw this, he said to himself, "If this man were a prophet, he would know who is touching him and what kind of woman she is…that she is a sinner."

Jesus answered him, "Simon, I have something to tell you." "Tell me, Teacher," he said. "Two men owed money to a certain money-lender. One owed him five hundred denarii, and the other fifty. Neither of them had the money to pay him back so he canceled the debts of both. Now which of them will love him more?" Simon replied, "I suppose the one who had the bigger debt canceled." "You have judged correctly," Jesus said.

Then he turned toward the woman and said to Simon, "Do you see this woman? I came into your house. You did not give me any water for my feet, but she wet my feet with her tears and wiped them with her hair. You did not give me a kiss, but this woman, from the time I entered, has not stopped kissing my feet. You did not put oil on my head, but she has poured perfume on my feet. Therefore, I tell you, her many sins have been forgiven…for she loved much. But he who has been forgiven little loves little."

Then Jesus said to her, "Your sins are forgiven."

Luke 7:36-48

I believe Jesus did something extraordinary for her, for her to show such open adoration. Perhaps He saved her from being stoned, as they did stone women caught in sexual sin. She wouldn't have spent the money to buy the expensive perfume, barged into a dinner without being invited, especially a religious leader's home. And then she let down her hair which was strictly forbidden in that culture unless she was in the privacy of her home. She did NOT care what they thought. Her overflowing gratitude could not be contained.

- What speaks to you in this passage?
- How do you identify with her? Or with Simon?
- How can you focus on gratitude for what He has done and let go of your past or what other people think of you?

Forgiveness Exercises

Scripture Meditation

Forgiveness is presented throughout the old and new testaments. Jesus tells us in the Lord's Prayer to. . . *forgive us our sins as we forgive those who sin against us.* (Luke 11:4) Other scripture references include: Matt. 6:12-15, Matt. 18:21-35, Mark 11:25, Luke 17:3, Eph. 4:32.

Some offenses are easy to forgive while other offenses take time. I don't like it when someone just throws a scripture at me. What is more helpful is to me is to meditate on a scripture and allow God to help me with the process. I encourage you to do that with these verses.

Write a Letter to the person

Pamela: *Even though my father was dead, I needed to write him a letter and tell him exactly how I felt. I l left nothing out. Then I was able to release it all, tear it up and throw it away. I can now say to my father that I really do look forward to seeing him in again. Our relationship will be renewed and restored.*

Writing a letter to the person who wounded you is very healing, even if the person is deceased.

- Tell them exactly how you felt and leave nothing out.
- Write until you get it all out.
- When you are ready to forgive, rip the letter into shreds and throw it away.

If you feel led to send it to the person, who is still alive, I would pray and seek wise counsel first.

_____
_____
_____
_____
_____
_____
_____
_____
_____
_____
_____
_____

Write a Letter to God

Jane: *Getting angry at God has been helpful in dealing with my son's death.*

Neil Anderson says that we need to forgive God.[35] You may be thinking, "What? God doesn't sin. He didn't cause the abuse. He is not responsible for my mistakes or my sin!" You are right and Neil would agree. What he means by that is not holding anything against God for what happened to you.

David lamented to God, and he was a man after God's heart. God is a BIG God and He can take it. He wants us to be authentic with Him. Since He already knows when we are angry with Him, it is for our sake to express it with Him.

After I lament to Him, I can begin to let go of Him not protecting me from the abuse or not stopping some tragedy in my life or whatever. I believe in Isaiah 55:5-8, that His thoughts and ways are higher than my thoughts and ways. Romans 8:28 tells me that all things work together for good even though I may not see it nor understand it. God is the master puzzle piece maker. I can only see the pieces that I fit into to. But God sees the whole finished puzzle. And it is good.

> My God, my God, why have you forsaken me?
>
> Psalm 22:1
>
> (Quoted by Jesus in Matthew 27:46 and Mark 15:34.)

Or see the Anger at God lament in Chapter 2.

Write a letter to God: _____

_____

_____

_____

_____

_____

_____

_____

_____

_____

_____

_

Here is a picture of what many believe is Golgotha or "The Skull" in Jerusalem. You can see the formation of the skull in the rock. My tour guide said that this was the place of punishment for years and believes Jesus was crucified in this place. I learned several other facts that I did not know. Jesus carried the horizontal portion of the cross since the vertical post (or tree) was already in the ground. He was put on the cross much lower than what we have seen in art. People were able to hear His last utterances from the cross which would have been difficult if He was up high. Evidence suggests the soldiers nailed the feet to either side of the post, driving the large stake through both feet. The Romans whipped the condemned before they were nailed to inflict the greatest amount of pain. The condemned were also stripped naked. Just knowing all this makes my stomach tie in knots. I can't imagine the severity of the pain He went through.

On the next page, is the Imaginative Prayer of Jesus and the Cross. You can use your imagination on what this would have looked like long ago.

Imaginative Prayer: The Cross, Luke 23:26-49

- Read the passage in Luke 23:26-49 slowly. Now close your eyes. Imagine you are there at the cross. What do you see? Hear? Smell?

- You are there with the other women, mourning. What are you mourning?

- As the soldiers crucified Him, Jesus says, "Father, forgive them, for they do onto know what they are doing." How does this speak to you?

- The thief on the cross asks Jesus to remember him. He does not ask for forgiveness or say the sinner's prayer. He did not do good works with his life and yet Jesus says to him, "I tell you the truth, today you will be with me in paradise." What does this scene reveal to you?

- Jesus looks at the disciple John standing there with His mother. He says, "Dear woman, here is your son," and to John, "Here is your mother." In other words, He asks John to take care of His mother. (I notice how Jesus honored His mother and yet did not ask one of His siblings to take care of her.) What do you think this means? (John 19:26-27). Here Jesus is dying, in extreme pain, and caring for someone other than Himself. How do you react to this?

- Jesus says, "I am thirsty." (John 19:28). What are you thirsty for?

- Jesus cries out, "My God, My God, why have you forsaken me?" (Mark 15:34-35). How do you relate?

- Finally, Jesus says, "Father, into your hands I commit my spirit." He takes His last breath. Be in silence for a while.

- Now try being someone else in this passage. Perhaps you are the thief next to Him. What do you need to say to Him? How do you feel about being in paradise with Him? Imagine the thief on the other side of Jesus is someone you need to forgive.

- Or perhaps you are one of the soldiers who are doing their job. Imagine casting lots for His cloak? One of the centurions did end up saying Jesus was a righteous man. I wondered how he felt about putting an innocent man to death.
  What is going on inside of you?

- Try being John or Jesus' mother or Mary Magdalene. These three were very close to Jesus and He loved them deeply as they did Him.

- When you are ready, imagine kneeling or laying down before the cross. Forgive those who hurt you whether they knew what they were doing or not. Receive His forgiveness.

- Express gratitude that you will be with Him in paradise.

Letting Go of the Ignorant

Sometimes people say things that are deeply hurtful. I believe most people do not intentionally try to cause harm with their words. They just are ignorant of what to say and what not to say. Sadly, these comments can contribute to the survivor's shame and inability to process and heal. When someone once said, "Well, that wasn't a big deal" to me then I just continued to minimize what happened to me. The first person who said, "I am so sorry that happened to you" was my therapist. With her compassion, I was able to explore what I really felt about my experience and open up about how it truly affected me. I say this to women when I listen to their story for the first time and they tell me, "No one has ever said that to me before." Yes, people just don't know what to say. So here is what to say and what not to say, based on my experience and on what the women you have met in this book have shared with me.

What not to say:

- "Oh, that happened so long ago."
- "You are over it now?"
- "I can't believe you are still hanging onto that."
- "Get over it."
- "I know how you feel." (no two people feel the same way)
- "Well there was no intercourse, so yours wasn't so bad." (comparing)
- "Oh, that explains why you are this way." (Ouch!)
- "Why are you doing this?" (Not Alone)
- "Do you think you were in some sexual sin so this is why this happened to you?"
- "What were you wearing?"
- "Are you sure you are not just making this up?"
- "Well, I don't think that is something to talk about."
- "You'll be fine. You can handle it."
- "I think you are being a bit dramatic."
- "Well, my childhood was wonderful…" (don't interrupt and make it about you)
- "You just need to forgive and move on."
- "You are called to forgive those who persecute you."
- "I hope you are praying for your parents."
- "Pray more." (Don't throw a scripture at someone)
- "God will take care of it."
- "It will be ok." (Don't try to cheer them up)
- Dead silence, and then change the subject.

What to say:

- "I am so sorry that happened to you."
- "What a painful experience for you."
- "I am sorry you had to experience that."
- "I can't imagine how you must feel."
- "What happened?" (Be respectful if one chooses not to share)
- "Would you like to talk about it?"
- "Share what is ever comfortable for you."
- "How do you feel about this?"
- "The abuse was not your fault."
- "Where is God with you in this?" (when timing is right)
- "I am here for you."
- "I am so proud of your courage, process, using your voice etc." (when timing is appropriate).
- Be Silent. Present. Compassionate. Listen. Make eye contact.
- Honor the person's story and vulnerability.
- Keep what is shared confidential. Treat it as sacred.

Reflection:

What are some helpful things people have said to you?

_____

_____

_____

What are some hurtful things that people have said to you? _____

_____

_____

_____

Sit and talk to God about the helpful sayings. Thank God for this person(s). Hear what God has to say to you.

Now sit and talk to God about the hurtful saying. Is there anyone you still feel anger and hurt towards? Were they intentional or ignorant? When you are ready, say the prayer below:

Prayer: As Jesus prayed on the cross: *Father, forgive them for they not know what they do…*

You pray: *Father, forgive _____ for they know not what they say.*

Letting Go of a Grudge

I was preparing to teach at a retreat on holding a grudge. So God, with his sense of humor, got in my face. I was holding a grudge against someone. I went to a show with reserved seats. In walks the person I was holding a grudge against. I could feel she was upset with me, too. There was an empty seat next to me. I said under my breath, "That better not be her seat next to mine." Well, guess what? It was. I was surprised that I started laughing inside. I said a few breath prayers. We talked cordially and parted kindly. The next day as I reflected, I found myself miffed at God. After a few minutes of griping, I genuinely asked God to help me let her go, let this grudge go. I did not want any of that ugly resentment in my being. Once I went through the following practice, I was able to let it go. I can honestly say that I am now able to pray for her and wish for God's best for her.

In my experience with others doing this practice, some were ready to invite the person to sit next to them and others were not. Some just had them stand there at the imaginary entrance. Please give yourself permission to be where you are at with forgiving this person. One woman stated that the person who stood at the door was a man from her past who called her a slut. She had forgotten this incident until God revealed this to her. She realized she had been believing that lie. She felt freer that day in group after we did this practice.

- Imagine a place that is safe for you (beach, garden, your house, the theater). Breathe in and out slowly. Feel the comfort, peace and safety this place offers you.
- Now you see God the Father or Jesus enter this place. He sits next to you. If you are comfortable, allow Him to put his arm around you. Soak in His love.
- Now you see this person whom you are holding a grudge against enter the room. Take a few moments to tell Jesus how the person hurt you. Hold nothing back.
- Hear Him understand and validate your feelings. What is He saying to you?
- Jesus asks *if you are ready* to invite the other to join you. *If yes*, invite him or her to sit on His other side. *If not*, they can stay at the entrance or at a distance.
- As you gaze at this person, try to see a child of God with wounds, strengths, weaknesses, and a work in progress. Try to see him or her as His beloved.
- Tell the person or Jesus something you learned or perhaps how you have grown even though the incident was painful.
- *If you are ready*, release the one who hurt you to God. Ask Him to help you forgive.
- Now it is time for the one who hurt you to leave. *If you are able*, pray for the person as you watch him or her walk away. Jesus gently says, *"Pray for your enemies."*
- Now turn back to God and express gratitude for His grace for you. Sit for a few more moments soaking in His love until it is time to go.

Forgiving Yourself

Many women get stuck here. They believe the wounding was their fault. Children especially tend to blame themselves. I thought what happened to me at the Berger's house was my fault. I felt guilty for not telling on him.

Amber: *I thought it was my fault because I was wearing a gypsy costume when my neighbor molested me.*

Maddison: *I thought I was to blame because it felt good. Then I learned our bodies were made to respond to pleasure but not to abuse.*

Let this message soak in: **IT WAS NOT YOUR FAULT.**

The abuse was not your fault. The wounding was not your fault. However, our choices, failings, manifestations, addictions, idols and sin, are our responsibility. We need to forgive ourselves or accept forgiveness for our part.

Missy: *It is not fair to look back and judge that woman or girl you were with the eyes of age and the wisdom of a new woman in Christ. Jesus didn't do this. He died on the cross and we are forgiven. It's over. So when you do judge yourself, you are denying what he did for you on the cross. Satan does this "Let's go down memory road" trap with you. Be careful of which route you take. Look at the facts. Would I do or say something differently? If you can say yes, without doubt or shame, then that is from God. If you feel shame and doubt, then that is from Satan. We can't control what another person does or how they respond. We can choose what we do and how we respond.*

Forgiving Yourself

This is something Missy has used in therapy with Christian clients. She states that for most women it takes a while to get here and to be ready to enter in. This exercise is to be done very slowly. You may want to do this with a mentor, counselor or spiritual director.

- Close your eyes. Relax. Breathe deeply for a few minutes and then breathe normally. Feel your body in the chair.
- Now imagine you are at a safe, enjoyable place (beach, mountains, desert, backyard, etc.). Use your senses. Feel the wind, the sun on your skin, the temperature. Make the place perfect for yourself.
- Now you see Jesus coming toward you. You watch Him as He walks toward you. He is looking right at you. He comes and sits down next to you. If it feels ok for you, allow Him to envelope you with His arms.
- Do you feel your cheek against His robe?
- Can you feel the warmth of His skin?
- Listen to His heart beating.
- Relax in the safety of His arms.

- After a few minutes, you listen to Him say these words to you:

"I love you my child"

"I love you just the way you are"

"You were created by my father"

"You are fearfully and wonderfully made"

"I know your feelings of fear, loneliness, pain, sorrow . . . and I am here to carry those burdens"

"The abuse was not your fault"

"I forgive you for everything"

"I will never leave you"

"You are precious to me"

- Just soak in his love.

- Then after a time, come back into the present, back into the room. Feel your body in the chair. Listen to your breathing. When you are ready, open your eyes.

Forgiving and Letting Go: The Model of Jesus

Jesus is the ultimate example of forgiveness. He was the ultimate sacrifice for our sins. On the cross, He forgave the soldiers who didn't even ask Him (Luke 23:34).

He didn't hold anything against His hometown people of Nazareth when they rejected Him. Even though that might have hurt Him, He moved on. He did not get His identity in his family of origin and how they treated Him. He knew who He was and followed His call (Luke 4:14-30).

With the woman caught in adultery, He told those to cast the first stone if they were without sin. He told her to sin no more and offered her freedom (John 8:1-11).

He offered freedom to Samaritan woman at the well. He spoke truth about her past and yet did not shame her (John 4). Instead He offered her Living Water.

He loved both Mary and Martha. He didn't beat Martha up for being busy; He was commenting on her choice at the time. Mary chose what was better in that moment which was to let go of busyness and sit at his feet (Luke 10:38-42).

He forgave the thief on the cross who did not do good works while he was on earth. He offered him paradise (Luke 28:43).

He forgave the paralytic and restored his ability to walk (Mark 2:5).

He hung out with the "sinners" of that time. He forgave them and partied with them (Mark 2:15-17).

He healed and forgave many people who came to Him in faith.

He didn't beat up any of the other disciples for falling asleep on Him in the garden, for abandoning him and fleeing in fear. Only John was there at the cross. The others hid in fear behind a locked door. And they were with Him for three years! They saw all the miracles, listened to His teachings and experienced His love. And they still left Him when He needed them most. And what did Jesus do?

He showed them grace. He appeared to them after the resurrection. He even fixed them breakfast by the Sea of Galilee (John 21:12). He filled them with His Holy Spirit fulfilling His promise of *I am always with you.*

He didn't criticize Thomas for doubting. Instead He let him put his hand in His wounds (John 20:27).

And He said blessed are those who believe, who have not seen, not experienced Him, like they did. And that is you and me (John 20:29).

Jesus forgave Peter for denying him. He drew Peter back into a loving relationship. (John 21:15-19). Such a beautiful story of reconciliation.

I believe Jesus forgave Judas who did feel remorse for betraying Him. Judas couldn't accept forgiveness like Peter and the others did.

He shows you grace. He does not beat you up. He does not continue to condemn you. He doesn't keep bringing up your past. It is done. It is over. Stop. Let it go. Forgive yourself.

He helps us pray for our enemies, including those who have wounded us. He helps us forgive and to not to take revenge or wish ill-will upon them.

Jesus did not have a "victim" mentality. He did not say, "Oh poor me, look what happened to me, I had to suffer, I was mocked and beaten then nailed to a tree," and so on. Yes, he suffered deeply for us and yet He didn't stay there. When He was resurrected, the scars from his wounds were still there and yet they were healed.

He used His wounds to reach out and help others. He knew who He was and was grounded in His identity. He didn't let the past wounds hold Him back.

Forgiveness is a process. I have been able to let go of those who have hurt me in my life, especially Mr. Berger and my dad. There have been others as well, as pain is inevitable if we are going to have relationships. I have asked forgiveness from those I know I have hurt as well. It helped me to understand what forgiveness is and what it is not. Sometimes we can let go quickly, other times its very slow like 77 x 7! And that is ok.

I encourage you to forgive yourself and stop beating yourself up for the past. If you feel the need, find a therapist, mentor or spiritual director to come along side as you try various forgiveness exercises shared in this chapter. What I hear from others and myself is that when I let go, I have more internal peace. That stinking video isn't playing in my head. When I forgive others and myself, I am the one who benefits. The greatest benefit is to live in freedom as the Beloved.

He helps me forgive, let go, take courage and step out. My wounds do not define who I am. I do not have a "victim" mentality and I am learning to be free to be me . . . to love and free to serve Him out of that love. And He can do the same for you! As He looks upon you, can you see the big smile on His face?

Turn to Jesus. Like for the thief on the cross, it is never too late.

Summary

Amber: *I still get angry at times yet I am more aware of when and why I overreact. I have found healing in forgiving the boy who molested me and for my parents who did nothing. Being a part of Al-Anon has helped me experience more peace, more serenity in my life.*

Pamela: *Healing is a process and I am grateful that I know I am worthy. I have a purpose. Healing prayer, the power of forgiveness and replacing lies with truth has helped know I am loved. I practice taking thoughts captive to Christ. I feel more love for God, myself and others in my life.*

Maddison: *Life still brings pain and I am learning how to sit with my feelings. Being able to serve others, especially those who are poor and don't know Jesus, has been a part of my call. I want to share Jesus' love with others. I want to be his feet and hands which brings joy in my life.*

Nancy: *I still struggle with busy-ness and getting my identity in my work. Yet God is with me and I know I am loved by him. Knowing the scriptures has helped my healing process. I have more faith in God.*

Clara: *Healing prayer is a part of my life. Through a prayer companion, God helps me search the depths of my soul. At times, I still struggle with anger and yet am able to unpack it, feel it and let it go much easier. I can see more gentleness in my life with myself and with others.*

Mariah: *I still struggle with anger and yet I know I have a voice. I speak up for what is right.*

Joy: *I don't let fear hold me back like it used to. I have more confidence now to step out and make a difference with my life.*

Missy: *God has healed me of my shame. Even though I still struggle with intimacy, I know I am forgiven and don't beat myself up for my past.*

Jane: *God is with me in my grief. It comes and goes. I will never get over the loss of my son but am able to get through it with His help.*

Beth: *My husband can see a difference in me. I have experienced the power of forgiveness. I still want to be in control, but now I am able to let things go much easier.*

Jesus said He came to give us life and give it abundantly. Life has its hardships and yet we can experience more of the internal fruits of the spirit: **love, joy, peace, patience, kindness, gentleness, goodness, faithfulness and self-control.** (Galatians 5:22). This kind of life is offered to all. I am grateful to have shared these precious stories with you. Each woman is unique, beautifully knit together, created as the beloved daughter of God. All have been wounded and all have experienced healing by God in their own way. We still struggle with issues as life has its ups and down. In the midst of trials, can live in a place of freedom, of being our true selves more often than not.

I hope you will continue to spend time with God, practicing the various spiritual disciplines, prayers, and exercises that allow His loving transformation. He loves you extravagantly and desires a relationship with you more than you know. He longs for you to become the beautiful woman he created you to be and live free as the Beloved.

Photograph by Katie Richardson, Australia 2012. Used with permission.

- What is this picture saying to you?

Let's re-visit the Woman at the Well. Here is the end of her story.

> Just then his disciples returned and were surprised to find him talking with a woman. But no one asked, "What do you want?" or "Why are you talking with her?" Then leaving her water jar, the woman went back to the town and said to the people, "Come see a man who told me everything I ever did. Could this be the Christ? They came out of the town and made their way toward him.
>
> John 4:27-30 (NIV)
>
> Many of the Samaritans from that town believed in him because of the woman's testimony, "He told me everything I ever did." So when the Samaritans came to him, they urged him to stay with them, and he stayed two days. And because of his words many more became believers.
>
> John 4:39-41 (NIV)

This woman is one of my favorites in scripture. I can relate to her shame. Then she experienced Jesus, the Wounded Healer, and the Living Water and was forever changed. Her shame melted into joy. She even left her valuable water jug at the well and ran off to go tell others about her experience. That would be like me leaving my purse or iPhone at the well! Jesus ignored tradition by talking to her as she was a woman, a Samaritan, and a woman who had been immoral. She broke the rules, too, and he didn't condemn her for it. He went out of His way through the desert in Samaria, not to point out her sin but to show her compassion and give her living water. She was full of joy, full of love, that she let go of what other people thought of her and told others her story. And God shares her story with us in His Holy book.

Like her, I have experienced wounds and the healing power of the living water in my life. Words cannot express the joy and gratitude in my heart towards God. I have confidence now with my call. Some women tell me they are not called to share their story as it is quite painful. Give yourself permission to share what is comfortable or not share at all. Try not to let others tell you what to do. Only God is the one who calls you according to His will. We are all unique with our gifts and our call.

Remember to come back to the well, the place where you experience being the Beloved. The place you receive forgiveness…joy…the Living Water. Whenever you feel rejection or failure, return to that internal, safe place of being the Beloved. Whenever shame tries to creep back into your soul, remember you are worthy. You are His precious daughter. When fear holds you back, remember you have a voice. He will give you strength and courage. When worry and anxiety dominate your mind, zapping your energy, go back to being in His presence in the moment. Let go of your control and whatever is blocking you from loving

God. Grieve what was lost while expressing gratitude for the gifts you have. Let go of the past. Forgive yourself. Above all, remember He loves you...more than you will ever know!

Thank you for journeying with me. I pray you will continue on this journey, becoming more of the Beloved every day. He loves you deeply and with you always!

As Jesus said to the bleeding woman, "Daughter, go in peace."

Appendix I
Leader's Guide

I would like to offer suggestions on how to run a *Not Alone* recovery group. As the leader, you can decide what time schedule works best for you.

Prior to starting a group, I have those who are interested fill out an application. An example is provided in Appendix II. I want to ensure the applicant is emotionally ready, able to make a commitment, and has had some kind of therapy or 12-step program. I also explain the process to them to determine if this is something they are looking for and to ensure the applicant is not in crisis. Many women tell me they have not done a deep, experiential group like this before. This process is for women who have admitted their brokenness, done some kind of therapeutic or healing work and are ready to go deeper with God. I suggest meeting in person or even Skype or Facetime so you can determine if someone is ready and a good fit.

It is important to be aware of group safety. For example, if this is done in a church setting, you want to be sure women feel safe with the others in the group. I was once in a group where the leader did not ensure safety and several of us "shut down." I do not push people to respond as this is not a therapy group. I do create a safe place where women are encouraged to share whatever is comfortable. My experience is that most women in group share very deeply from their hearts.

I find 3-6 is the right number of applicants to accept in a group. Larger than 8 can start to feel too big and limit the amount of sharing. Many women have told me that they prefer a smaller group of 4-5.

Once our group is formed, I send a copy of Writing your Story (Appendix III) ahead of time. I ask the women to be prepared to share their story on the first day. Depending on the size of the group, I give them 10 min. to present. I share my story first. I do believe women will be more vulnerable when the leader is. After sharing stories, I go over "Creating the Space Inside and Outside of Group".

I find two hours is a good length of time for each individual session. This allows enough time for sharing about their experience with God, teaching, and doing a practice together in group. As far as overall length of time, you can do this group in several ways. I meet every week for three weeks in the beginning and then meet every other week. I really stress an every other week rhythm. This gives them more time to do the practices with God. I stress the key to this process is time spent with God as He is the healer, the one who transforms. Even two weeks is not really enough time for the healing practices, since transformation is a lifelong process, but at least this is better than meeting once a week and rushing through it.

Usually on our second meeting, we create a covenant agreement together, which I type up. Then we all sign it and receive a copy. I find this gives each woman ownership of her part and commitment to the group. I have an example of one in Appendix IV.

I have done this group in 10 sessions and in 12 sessions, usually starting in January and ending in June. Another option is to do 5-6 sessions in the fall and then another 6-7 sessions in the winter-spring. If time, I have offered an additional final meeting where we get out in nature or meet at a retreat center and have a closing ceremony together.

I provide a lot of materials. I have found its best to have a variety of practices to offer since we all connect in different ways with God. I tell them to try as many practices as they can and then choose what works for them. For every woman who says she does not like a certain practice, another says she loves it. This is why I provide many to choose from. As the leader, you can choose which practice to do together during group time. The rest can be done at home.

When you do a practice in group, the key is to **read the scripture and the questions slowly**. Give space and silence for God to enter in. During Imaginative Prayer, I allow at least two minutes of silence after for each question I ask. It's so important that you as the leader are comfortable with silence. This silent space is where God enters in. I have witnessed many amazing encounters these women have had with God in silence. Often (not always) they will hear from Him or experience His love or gain insight. Tears are common when His Holy Spirit moves.

Please don't try to get in all the teaching and stories in every session. It's better to do less…slowly…than try to fit in everything. There is too much information to get it all in. I pray and seek wisdom prior to every session to decide what practice to do in group, depending on how the group is going. Since silence is difficult for most people, I usually choose the Imaginative prayer or a meditation type of practice. The women can do the Reflections and read most of at it home in the quiet space with God. I also do a teaching on each chapter.

Here is an example of the flow of group in a given session:
- First 45 minutes: have the women share their experiences of God since the last meeting and any insight from the materials from previous session.
- Next 30 minutes: teach on the current chapter.
- Next 30 minutes: do a practice together and then share about experience. (It's ok if they didn't feel anything. Most women do).
- Last 15 minutes: wrap-up and closing.

Please feel free to contact me at my website: www.spiritualdirectionandtrauma.com if you have questions or need assistance. May God bless you and the women you journey with!

Appendix II
Application for Group

Group Member Information

Please complete some general information for group membership for *Not Alone*. This information will be confidential and useful for us to ensure safety and optimum connection within the group. Please send to (your name) at:_____.

Name: _____

DOB: _____

Address: _____
_____

Email: _____

Phone: _____

Emergency Contact: _____
_____

Please briefly describe, whatever is comfortable to share about the trauma (ex. childhood abuse, sexual trauma, emotional abuse, domestic violence):
_____
_____
_____
_____

Professional counseling/therapy:
_____
_____

Other support or faith-based groups (12 step, AA, Al anon, healing prayer, etc.):
_____
_____

What do you hope to gain from this group?
_____
_____

Are you able to commit to the days/time? _____

I believe that Jesus is the Wounded Healer and am asking each member to spend at least 30 minutes each day with Him to do the prayer practices and reflections. Will you be able to do your best? _____

Any other information you'd like to share with facilitator:

_____

_____

_____

_____

Signature: _____

Date: _____

Appendix III
Writing Your Story

I encourage to write out your story. The purpose is twofold. First, to help you see how God has been present throughout your life even when you did not see it or feel it. The second is to prepare to share your story in group or with your spiritual director/mentor. Sharing stories is healing in and of itself. It helps us see that we are not alone. We gain insight from one another. As I mentioned before, share what you are comfortable with about the trauma. I would suggest a minimum of five pages and no more than eight. Try not to write too many details; just focus on the significant events and people in your life, especially those that influenced your image/belief in God. Consider the following:

- Describe your home growing up. What was it like?
- Describe your parents. What were they like? What messages did you receive from them about life and the world?
- Describe your siblings. What were they like?
- Any other significant relatives (e.g. grandparents, etc.)?
- Write about what stood out in your school years. Who was your favorite teacher? Your least favorite teacher? What did you learn about yourself or God through both of them?
- What did you learn about God through church, Sunday school, or clergy?
- Write about any significant mentors in your life. What did you learn about God from them?
- Write about major milestones: graduation, career, marriage, children, grandchildren, retirement, etc. How have these influenced your spiritual life?
- Include the 3-4 best events/experiences in your life.
- Include the 3-4 most painful experiences in your life.

Reflect on the best things/events in your life. Then answer the following questions:

- How did you experience God during these best times?
- How was God there?
- Where was God leading you through that situation?
- What did you learn? How have your grown?
- Was there a turning point in your faith?
- As you reflect, express gratitude for all the gifts and answered prayer (both big and small) God gave you during the best times.

Reflect on the painful times/event of your life. Ask yourself the same questions above.

- How did you experience God during these times?
- Can you try to see how He was there even though you may not have felt it?
- Is God safe for you?
- Was there a turning point in your faith?
- What did you learn through the hard times?
- Are you able to trust Him with your current situation? Why or why not?
- In your own words, express gratitude for how you survived, how you were able to get through and to God for being there with you.

Appendix IV

Covenant Agreement for Not Alone

I will keep what is shared in this group confidential. Although I can share my own stories with others, I will keep my peers' comments confidential, for the sake of others, unless I have written permission to share another person's story.

I will be on time.

I will commit to the time frame and not be absent unless it's absolutely necessary (illness, planned vacation, major problem).

If I miss more than two sessions, I acknowledge that I will not be able to return as regular attendance is necessary to maintain group safety.

I will commit to most of the homework. I will be open and try the different spiritual practices with God in the space I have created.

I will be kind, encouraging and compassionate with myself and with others.

Signed: _____

Personal contact info: _____

_____

_____

Acknowledgements

First, I would like to thank my husband, Ron, who helped me with formatting and editing this material. He created the space and support for me to create this book. I couldn't have done it without him.

My family has been a tremendous support and I thank Ron and my daughter, Katie, for the beautiful photos they took that are presented in the book and on the covers.

I would also like to thank my editor, Vicki Hesterman, for her encouragement and skill in editing my materials. Her knowledge of the publishing process allowed me to complete all the necessary tasks to make this book happen. I also appreciated the beautiful job she did with the cover design.

I would like to thank Karen Ritter, LCSW, for coming along side me with presenting the first *Not Alone* group in her office. I appreciated her insights and contributions to my book as a psychotherapist.

I want to thank my first spiritual director Caralie Norman for all the teachings and practices, some which I have shared in this book. I appreciate my second spiritual director, Sister Bunny Flick, for believing in my call to write this book and minister to women who have had trauma.

I am so grateful for my soul group: Ann Whitely, Nanette Ayers and Mary Linam who have listened, prayed and encouraged me along the way. They have been a wonderful support.

Most of all I am so grateful for all the *hers:* the women who have journeyed with me in Spiritual Direction and in *Not Alone.* They have shared their precious stories, their pain and their joy with me. I have witnessed God's loving transformation in their lives. I am so honored to come along side in their healing journey.

Endnotes

Chapter 1

1. St. Ignatius (1491-1556). Fleming, David, SJ (2011) *Draw me Into Your Friendship: The Spiritual Exercises*. Saint Louis, Missouri. The Institute of Jesuit Sources, p.100

Chapter 2

2. Prayer of Examen. Fleming, David, SJ (2011) *Draw me Into Your Friendship: The Spiritual Exercises*. Saint Louis, Missouri. The Institute of Jesuit Sources, p. 28-29
3. Fleisher, Sheryl, Unpublished exercise: "Practicing Joy," used with permission, October 10, 2018.
4. Quinn, Mike. Lead pastor and founder of Newbreak Church, San Diego.
5. Gallagher, Timothy (2015) *Discerning the Will of God: An Ignatian Guide to Christian Decision Making*. The Crossroad Publishing Company.
6. Anderson, Neil T. (1990) *The Bondage Breaker*. Eugene, Oregon. Harvest House Publishers. California.

Chapter 3

7. Young, WM Paul, (2007) *The Shack*. Newbury Park, CA 91320. Windblown Media Publishing.
8. Warner, Larry. Spiritual Director, Founder of b-ministries (www.b-ing.org.) Unpublished exercise: "Image of God," used by permission, Oct. 27, 2018.
9. Paintner, Christine Valters (2011) *Lectio Divina- the Sacred Art: Transforming Words and Images into Heart-Centered Prayer*. Woodstock, VT. SkyLight Paths Publishing.

Chapter 4

10. Anderson, Neil, (p. 47) 1992 Freedom in Christ Ministries, Neil Anderson, *Victory Over the Darkness*, Bethany House Publishers, a division of Baker Publishing group. Used by permission.

Chapter 5

11. Hoffman, Mary Byrne. Spiritual Director and Wellness Practitioner. San Diego, CA.
12. Culbreth, Sallie M.S. and Anne Quinn. *The Uncaged Project: Spiritual Strategies to Move Beyond Abuse*. Founder of Committed to Freedom Ministries.

Chapter 7

13. Springle, Pat (2003), *Untangling Relationships: A Christian Perspective on Codependency*. Houston, Texas. Rapha Publishing.
14. Keating, Thomas (2011) Centering Prayer , *Open Mind, Open Heart* 20th Anniversary edition, New York, NY. Continuum International Publishing Group.
15. Alcoholics Anonymous and Al-Anon, "Serenity Prayer."

Chapter 8

16. Twain, Mark, author, (1835-1910).
17. Ten Boom, Corrie (1892-1983), survivor of the Holocaust, author of *The Hiding Place*.
18. Julian of Norwich, English mystic and author (1342-1416).
19. McHugh, Joe, SJ, Instructor at Mercy Center Burlingame. Burlingame, California.
20. Lenell, Karen, retired MFT: Marriage and Family Therapist. San Diego, Personal communication.

Chapter 9

21. Ritter, Karen, LCSW. San Diego, California. Personal communication.
22. Lelwica, Michelle M. *The Religion of Thinness*. Gurze books.
23. Gungor, Marc, Pastor and creator of DVD series: *Laugh Your Way to a Better Marriage*.
24. Davis, Laura,(1990) *The Courage to Heal Workbook: For Women and Men Survivors of Child Sexual Abuse*. New York, NY. HarperCollins Publishers.
25. Finley, James, PhD (2018) *Standing Against Sexual Harassment and the Abuse of Power*. Unedited Transcript. Center of Action and Contemplation, New Mexico.

Chapter 10

26. Nouwen, Henri (1996) *The Inner Voice of Love*. New York, NY. Doubleday, a division of Random House, Inc.
27. Norman, Caralie (2008) "Healthy Rhythm in Relationships," Unpublished article, used by permission.
28. Cloud, Henry, PhD and Townsend, John, PhD. (1995) *Boundaries* Workbook. Orange, CA. Yates & Yates.
29. Cloud, Henry, PhD and Townsend, John, PhD. (1995) *Safe People*. Orange, CA. Yates & Yates Downers Grove, IL. InterVarsity Press.
30. Springle, *Untangling Relationships*.
31. Perry, Tyler, playwright, *Madea goes to Jail*, American musical play, touring 2005-2006.
32. Warren, Rick, lead pastor of Saddleback Church, Orange County, California.
33. Rohr, Richard (2011) *Falling Upward*. San Francisco, CA. Jossey-Bass Publisher.

Chapter 12

34. Fleisher, Sheryl (1985) *Forgiveness*. Unpublished. Used by permission.
35. Anderson, Neil T. (1990) *The Bondage Breaker*.

References

Allender, Dan B. with Lee-Thorp, Karen (2008) *The Wounded Heart: Hope for Adult victims of Childhood Sexual Abuse.* Navpress resource in alliance with Tyndale House Publishers, Inc.

Allender, Dan B. with Mullins, Traci (2016) *Healing the Wounded Heart Workbook: The Heartache of sexual abuse and the Hope of Transformation.* Grand Rapids, MI. Baker Books.

Anderson, Neil T. (1990) *Victory Over the Darkness.* Ventura, CA. Regal Books.

Anderson, Neil T. (1990) *The Bondage Breaker.* Eugene, Oregon. Harvest House Publishers.

Benner, David G. (2004) *The Gift of Being Yourself.* Downers Grove, IL. InterVarsity Press.

Benner, David G. (2003) *Surrender to Love.* Downers Grove, IL. InterVarsity Press.

Benner, Juliet (2011) *Contemplative Vision.* Downers Grove, IL. InterVarsity Press.

Bromley, Nicole Braddock (2009) *Breathe: Finding Freedom to Thrive in Relationships After Childhood Sexual Abuse.* Chicago, IL. Moody Publishers.

Bromley, Nicole Braddock (2007) *Hush: Moving From Silence to Healing After Childhood Sexual Abuse.* Chicago, IL. Moody Publishers.

Calhoun, Adele Ahlberg (2005) *Spiritual Disciplines Handbook: Practices that Transform Us.*

Cloud, Henry, PhD and Townsend, John, PhD. (1995) *Boundaries Workbook.* Orange, CA. Yates & Yates.

Cloud, Henry, PhD and Townsend, John, PhD. (1995) *Safe People.* Orange, CA. Yates & Yates Downers Grove, IL. InterVarsity Press.

Courage to Change (1992) Virginia Beach, VA. Al-Anon Family Group Headquarters, Inc.

Davis, Laura (1990) *The Courage to Heal Workbook: For Women and Men Survivors of Child Sexual Abuse.* New York, NY. HarperCollins Publishers.

Fleming, David, SJ (2011) *Draw me Into Your Friendship: The Spiritual Exercises.* Saint Louis, Missouri. The Institute of Jesuit Sources.

Foster, Richard (1998) *Celebration of Discipline: the Path to Spiritual Growth.* New York, NY 10022. HarperCollins Publishers.

Gallagher, Timothy (2015) *Discerning the Will of God: An Ignatian Guide to Christian Decision Making.* The Crossroad Publishing Company.

Keating, Thomas (2011) *Open Mind, Open Heart* 20th, Anniversary edition, New York, NY. Continuum International Publishing Group.

Lawrence, Brother. (1982) *The Practice of the Presence of God.* New Kensington, PA: Whitaker House.

May, Gerald G. (1998) *Addictions and Grace: Love and Spirituality in the Healing of Addictions.* New York, NY. HarperCollins Publishers.

McKay, Matthew, Ph.D, Fanning, Patrick, Church, Carole Honey, and Sutker, Catherine (2005) *The Self-Esteem Companion: Simple exercises to Help You Challenge Your Inner Critic and Celebrate Your Personal Strengths.* Oakland, CA. New Harbinger Publications, Inc.

Nouwen, Henri (1998) *The Inner Voice of Love.* New York, NY. Doubleday, a division of Random House, Inc.

Paintner, Christine Valters (2011) *Lectio Divina- the Sacred Art: Transforming Words and Images into Heart-Centered Prayer.* Woodstock, VT. SkyLight Paths Publishing.

Rohr, Richard (2011) *Falling Upward.* San Francisco, CA. Jossey-Bass Publisher.

Silf, Margaret (2004) *The Gift of Prayer.* New York, NY. BlueBridge.

Springle, Pat (2003) *Untangling Relationships: A Christian Perspective on Codependency.* Houston, Texas. Rapha Publishing.

Warner, Larry (2010) *Journey with Jesus: Discovering the Spiritual exercises of Saint Ignatius.* Downers Grove, IL. InterVarsity Press.

.

DVD Series: *Laugh Your Way to a Better Marriage* by Mark Gungor

CD Series: *Transforming Trauma* by James Finely, Ph.D.

Articles:

Norman, Caralie (2007) "Soaking in God's Love." Unpublished. Used by permission

Norman, Caralie (2008) "Healthy Rhythm in Relationships." Unpublished. Used by permission

Flesher, Sheryl (1985) "Forgiveness." Unpublished. Used by permission.

Made in the USA
Columbia, SC
08 July 2021